Two Who Survived

Two Who Survived

Keeping Hope Alive While Surviving the Holocaust

Rose and Max Schindler's story,
Written by M. Lee Connolly

TWO WHO SURVIVED

Published by

MRS
publishing

www.MRSPublishing.com

ISBN: 978-1-7329198-1-5 (Paperback)
ISBN: 978-1-7329198-7-7 (Hardcover)
ISBN: 978-1-7329198-0-8 (e-book)

Library of Congress Control Number: 2018968009

Edited by Rosalyn R. Hafner
Designed by Mary Adsit, AdsitDesign.com
Printed by Sustainable Print and Mail, San Diego, California

First Edition, Second Printing
May, 2020

Ordering Information: TwoWhoSurvived.com

Front Cover: Rose Schwartz and Max Schindler
on Brighton Palace Pier, UK, circa 1948-49

TABLE *of* CONTENTS

Dedicated to

We, Rose and Max, dedicate this book to the many individuals who helped us to rise from the ashes of the Holocaust, enabling us to prosper as a loving couple for nearly 70 years.

Thank you

Thank you to the liberating armies and individual soldiers who made a difference, to the medical personnel, the refugee assistance providers and resettlement agencies, we are forever grateful and humbled by your efforts.

We appreciate the United States of America, which has become our home. It has provided us, our children and grandchildren with countless blessings and opportunities.

Our deepest thanks and utmost gratitude go out to our writer M. Lee Connolly. Lee came to us after hearing Rose and Max speak one day in a classroom setting. Lee was inspired by Rose and Max, which eventually led to this book.

We also give heartfelt thanks to Mary Adsit who designed and produced this beautiful book and Rosalyn Hafner who brilliantly edited it and polished it up to perfection.

In Memory

We remember our many relatives murdered during the Holocaust. We will never forget the 6 million persons of Jewish descent, and the millions of others who perished during the course of WWII.

We implore you to remember. Read our true story and remember to speak out when you are a witness to another's suffering.

Never Forget!

This book is a compilation of memories from the lives of Rose and Max Schindler. Their stories begin when they are quite young and progress through their lives. Both Rose and Max tell their stories to the best of their ability, but admit that after over forty years of recounting these events, they remember some scenes more vividly than others. All of the stories contained in this book are accurate to the best of Rose and Max's knowledge, which has the unique benefit of having been repeated many, many times over the course of more than 40 years. The Schindlers make it their goal to give only an accurate recounting, and withhold anything that is uncertain in their minds. It is their strong belief that when they speak, they need to be accurate. When asked about why they continue to speak out, they both say:

"We need to learn and remember, so it will never happen again."

As you read this book, you become one of those who can learn and remember. Listen to their true stories with the ears of the inquisitive and a mind open to new understandings. Books allow us to run our own feature films in our mind. So, bring the lights down and open the screen to the feature film about Rose and Max. This "movie" is filled with experiences you may never have known before. Let the film run and imagine how you might be in similar circumstances. When the film is done and the lights come up, you will be transformed. You will be the one who can ensure that it never happens again, because now you know.

★ Berlin

GERMANY

★ Cottbus

Dresden
Zschachwitz ✡

Death March

Theresienstadt ✡
★ Prague

CZECHOSLOVAKIA

Bruntal

Brno

AUSTRIA

Vienna
★

✡ Auschwitz II-Birkenau, Poland - Extermination Camp
✡ Bedzieszyna, Poland - Slave Labor Camp
✡ Bruntal (Freudenthal), Czechoslovakia - Slave Labor Camp
★ Brzesko, Poland - Home of Max's paternal grandparents
★ Cottbus, Germany - Max's home
✡ Mielec, Poland - Slave Labor Camp

POLAND

✪ Warsaw

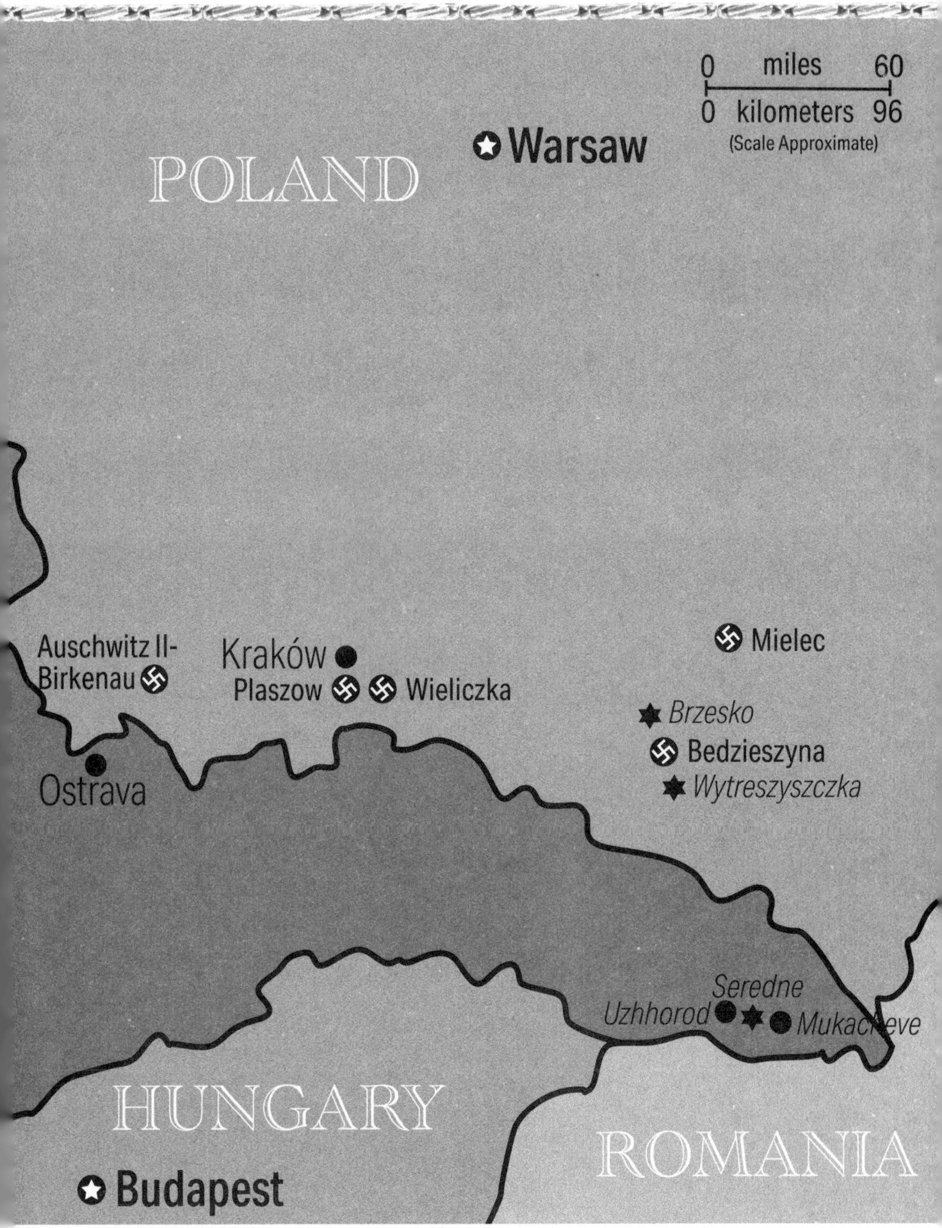

0   miles   60
0   kilometers   96
(Scale Approximate)

Auschwitz II-Birkenau 卐

Kraków ●

Plaszow 卐   卐 Wieliczka

卐 Mielec

★ *Brzesko*

卐 Bedzieszyna

★ *Wytreszyszczka*

Ostrava ●

Seredne
Uzhhorod ● ★ ● *Mukacheve*

HUNGARY

✪ Budapest

ROMANIA

卐   Plaszow, Poland - Concentration Camp
★   Seredne, Czechoslovakia - Rose's home
卐   Theresienstadt, Czechoslovakia - Ghetto & Concentration Camp
卐   Wieliczka, Poland - Slave Labor Camp
★   Wytreszyszczka, Poland - Home of Max's maternal grandparents
卐   Zschachwitz Factory - Dresden, Germany - Slave Labor Camp

Rose's father (with beard) in his tailor shop, Seredne, Czechoslovakia, circa 1937

CHAPTER ONE

Sweet Seredne, A Country Life: *Rose*

When the snow arrives in October, we love to go sledding on the hill near the ruined castle. There is a certain kind of snow that allows you to sled down the hill so fast, you feel like you are flying. It's a light, powdery snow that sparkles in the sun and falls like sifted flour when you toss it up. This isn't the best snow for snowball fights, but it's perfect for sledding. Today looks like one of those days.

We take two sleds because there are eight of us kids. My father, called Tata, and my older brother, Fischel, built our sleds from wood. We all love sledding, even when a sled tips over, which always happens at some point. We roll or bounce off the sled

1

and come up giggling, covered in snow. We brush the powdery snow off each other's woolen coats and clap our hands together to knock snow off our mittens. Occasionally there are tears from one of us, but that quickly stops when someone yells, "Let's go again!"

The older kids have to drag the sleds back up the hill, because I am too small. Trudging up that hill over and over again keeps us warm in the cold weather, so we continue sledding for hours. The snow falls from October through April, giving us plenty chances for sledding.

My name is Roysie (Rose) Schwartz. I am eight years old and in the third grade. I like to tell stories. I was born on December 28, 1929, the fourth child in a family of six girls and two boys. Hiyasura (Helen) is 15, Yutke (Judy) is 13, Fischel (Philip) is 11, Petyu is five, Blimchu is three, Fay is two and Myerbear is just a baby. Momma's name is Regina or Rifka and Tata's name is Solomon or Shlomo Zalman. Not all families have eight kids, but many do. I know families that have fourteen children, so our family is not too big. Momma says our family, with grandparents, cousins, aunts and uncles, has more than 100 people. This makes Momma and Tata very proud.

My family lives in Czechoslovakia, and we learn to speak Czech in school. Momma and Tata learned Hungarian in school when they were my age. After World War I, in 1918, the government changed from the Austro-Hungarian Empire to democratic Czechoslovakia. Sometimes when the government changes, the official language does too. That is when our language changed from Hungarian to Czech. Since it is now 1937, it's been almost 20 years and Tata says everyone is used to speaking in Czech.

My parents say the Czech government is good to us. Everyone has equal rights and my family does all we can to be good citizens. Neighbors help each other and are always friendly. We speak Hungarian or Czech with our friends. Ukrainian is a similar language that is spoken by many, so we speak this also. And because we are Jewish, we speak Yiddish, the language of our faith, at home. My brother goes to Cheder (religious school for children) to learn Hebrew. Girls don't have to go to Cheder or learn Hebrew, and that is good with me. Speaking many languages is not unusual for my family and friends.

One time I asked my father, "Tata, why do we speak so many languages?" He sat down with me to explain. He told me that we live beneath the Carpathian Mountains. This area has fertile land for our farm to grow vegetables. The giant forests supply us with wood for our fires. The rivers and streams are filled with fish. The orchards and vineyards give us fruit and wine. All these good things make our home a place where many different people want to live. Sometimes they fight over who is in charge. Hungarians live here and sometimes fight with Ukrainians. Some Germans have set up colonies here. Romanians, Turks, Slovaks, Czechs and Gypsies also live here. Each brings their own faith and language, like our Yiddish. Tata says that is why everyone speaks so many different languages here. He is so good at helping me understand why our life is this way. My father is wise, kind and always willing to answer all my questions.

Once, Hiyasura told me there was another baby in our family before we were born, but it died within a few days. Losing the baby was very hard for Momma and Tata. We don't talk about that baby. I think Hiyasura knows more about this because she is the oldest.

When it is time for a baby to be born, a midwife from the village comes to the home to help. She stays long enough after the baby is born to be sure the mother and baby are healthy. Momma had a housekeeper help her every day when the first few babies were born. Lots of families have housekeepers when babies are small, but not all families can afford one. The housekeepers sometimes need a place to live or work as a way to help their families. They cook and clean while the mothers care for their new babies.

As the first children grow older, they begin to help their parents more, so a housekeeper is no longer needed. Now that we are growing up, we don't need that help anymore.

My father's sister, Aunt Lea, lives with us. Her husband died in the First World War. When her only son was 17 years old, he decided to move to the Holy Land, leaving her by herself. Since she was alone, my parents invited her to live with our family. Aunt Lea is a seamstress, so she sews all our clothes. When one girl grows out of a dress, it goes to the next sister to use. We call these hand-me-downs. We are glad Aunt Lea lives with us because she is a friend for Momma, and helps take care of us kids.

It is part of our religion to always be kind to others. Momma and Tata taught us to be kind to our neighbors. Momma teaches us girls to become caring wives and Tata teaches the boys how to be good husbands. Boys also learn a trade so they can support their wives and families.

In the Jewish faith, young people are introduced to each other by a matchmaker who determines a good match and recommends a marriage. My parents were chosen for each other by a matchmaker. Momma lived several hours away by bus from Tata, when they were introduced. Momma and Tata liked each other when the introduction happened, so they agreed to a match. Tata was 23 and Momma was 19 when they got married. Luckily, they grew to love each other very much and are happy to have produced a large family.

Momma showed me her wedding picture where she and Tata both were smiling and dressed up all fancy. We don't have a lot of photographs at our house because no one has a camera. To get photographs, you need a traveling photographer to come and take your picture. It comes in the mail a few weeks later. This usually only happens at celebrations, like weddings.

Momma says we have many traditions that are unique to our religion. For example, as is customary, she shaved off her hair for the wedding and wore a wig. Women keep their hair short and under a wig in public, after marrying. At home they often wear a scarf to cover their head. I will shave my hair when I get married.

Momma and Tata are raising us as Orthodox Jews and we follow the rules faithfully. We always eat foods that are specially prepared to honor Jewish dietary laws called Kosher. Each week we celebrate Shabbat on Friday night, before the holy day on Saturday. We attend synagogue and speak Yiddish at home. We believe strongly that God will protect us from anything bad. Our code of conduct says that the way we act in life is how we show our faith.

My older sisters are finished with school, but I still go. Every weekday I walk to class with my brother Fischel and younger sister,

Petyu. We meet friends along the way. School is the only two-story building in town. Since it is just a short walk from home, we go home for lunch and then return to classes in the afternoon. We study math, reading, writing, and the Czech language. When we get out of school at 3:00 pm each day, it is a relief for me. I don't really like school, but I have to go.

On the way home, I get to relax and talk about things I am interested in. We speak Czech with our friends, or Yiddish if they are Jewish. I like to walk home with my friend Betty. Our classmates all know each other and have been going to school together for years. I do not like the homework that we do every evening after chores. I have three more years of school before I am done. Hiyasura loves books and wants to get a higher education. I don't want that. I think I will learn to be a seamstress when I grow up, so I can sew clothes for my family.

We have a comfortable, three-room home on Main Street. Our kitchen is the largest room of all. The kitchen oven is so big that I could lie down inside of it if I wanted to. Momma keeps all the pans, silverware, drinking glasses and dishes on top of the oven. It has a big space in the bottom for the wood fire that heats it. The neighbors sometimes come over to use our oven because they have only a small oven or don't have an oven at all.

In the kitchen, there is a long wooden table with benches on each side of it. It is long enough to fit the whole family and even a few guests. When people come to visit, they sit at the table to talk with Momma. She never sits down in the kitchen except to eat, because she is always busy cooking and preparing food.

On Fridays, Momma uses the big oven to bake for the whole week. The house fills with the wonderful smell of bread and sweets. Yutke says the smell of yeast and sugar baking is how she thinks heaven will smell. It always makes me feel happy. In winter, we love the feel of the heat from the oven door when we come in from the cold.

One of my favorite things Momma bakes is rye bread. When Momma allows us to have some of the warm bread with melting butter on it, I am the happiest girl anywhere. She bakes many loaves of bread to feed everyone during the week.

Momma bakes a delicious challah bread for our Shabbat dinner. She braids three pieces of dough like she braids our hair. It gets taller and fluffier as it bakes, and the center is as soft as a pillow. This bread tastes sweet and is beautiful to look at. Everyone looks forward to it. Momma also bakes sweet desserts for Shabbat that we all love.

Churning the butter for our bread is my chore. Pulling and pushing that stick in the barrel for hours is so hard, that sometimes it makes my arms feel like they are going to fall off. I really don't like this chore, but Momma says it is important so I know I can't complain. I guess it is worth the work because the butter tastes so wonderful on Momma's bread.

Momma is strict with us so we will learn how to live a good Jewish life, but she is also loving. Even when Momma scolds me, I know she is teaching me how to be good. I want to be like Momma when I grow up.

Because our family has many children, every room in our house has beds. The bed in the kitchen is at the far end, near the pantry. This is where my two brothers, Fischel and Myerbear, sleep. The living room has two beds where all six of us girls sleep. I sleep with Yutke and Fay in one bed. I don't mind because I am small so there is enough room. Fay needs a big girl to sleep next to her because she gets scared easily. Hiyasura sleeps with Petyu and Blimchu.

The third room in our house is Momma and Tata's room. They each get their own smaller bed and do not have to share like us kids. There is a nightstand with a kerosene lamp on it between the beds. They also have a couch in their room where we can sit and talk to Momma while she folds clothes or hangs them in the wardrobe. Winter coats and clean dresses go in there. When I grow out of my clothes, Momma says I can shop in the wardrobe. It is fun to go hunting for a new dress in the dark, deep wardrobe.

Most of the clothes we wear in the winter are made from wool because it is so cold. It is especially cold at night, so all the beds have cozy warm quilts on them. Momma sews the quilts and fills them with goose down feathers. She is a very good seamstress. It is hard work plucking feathers from a goose, but Yutke, Hiyasura and I are good at it. The down feathers make the quilts snuggly warm. Our pillows are also filled with goose down feathers which makes them soft. Each bed has a mattress made from a burlap bag filled with straw, that makes them comfortable to sleep on.

Every night, we light the house with kerosene lanterns that give the house a golden glow and a special smell. We are cozy and warm in our house on the cold winter nights. In the summer months, we open the windows to let the heat out, and a fresh breeze comes in.

When it is time to go to sleep, we place our shoes under the beds and put on our night clothes from under the pillows. We lay out the clothes we just removed for the next day, then climb under the quilt. We always giggle a little under the covers to get the last of our energy out before we fall asleep. When Momma turns out the kerosene lamp hanging from the ceiling, our room gets pitch black. Fay is a little afraid of the dark, so she snuggles up close to me.

Our living room is always warm from cooking dinner on the stove in the corner. I am glad to sleep in the room with the stove since it can get so cold on winter nights.

We use the living room for special meals, like Shabbat. It is big enough for a second table with benches all around it. The rest of the time we eat in the kitchen.

Outside of the house and near the garden are the water pump and the outhouse. It's a little stinky in there but Momma says it's better to go out there than in here, as she points to the floor in the house. When we are done, we just go to the pump to wash up.

Our water pump is a modern metal hand pump, that pumps water up to the spigot every time you push the handle down. Momma keeps two kinds of water in the house. One type is for washing and the other type is for cooking and drinking. Some of our neighbors still have a well with a bucket that lifts water up. Sometimes things fall into those wells, so wells are scary to me. Our pump is newer and safer. No one can fall in it.

In the cold winter months, I don't like having to put on layers of clothes to go outside to the outhouse. If I get up in the night, I just use an old bucket to relieve myself and jump right back in bed. I empty the bucket in the morning.

Our home and all our neighbors' homes are farms. Most of my Jewish friends live in the homes on Main Street. It takes a few minutes to walk to our next-door neighbor's house because of the big gardens and fields we all have. We have plenty to eat each day and most of it grows on our farm. All of us kids help Momma manage the animals and the vegetables. Momma says our farm is one acre, but to me it feels as big as a whole meadow.

Yutke and Momma milk the cows every morning, filling a shiny metal bucket with warm milk. The bucket sits underneath our mother cow, while they squeeze the milk free from her udders. Momma says it is relaxing to milk the cow, but I am not good at it. It takes a long time for me to fill a bucket with milk, one squirt at a time. Momma knows how to make buttermilk, cheese and cottage cheese from the cow's milk. I love to drink the milk in our coffee every morning.

I help tend to the garden and collect eggs. Picking up eggs from the chickens is a little tricky because you can't drop them. You have to be careful how you hold the basket of eggs too, because one egg can roll and crack another egg or even fall out of the basket. I am good at protecting the eggs.

One chore I like is pulling up potatoes. They only grow once a year, but they last a long time, stored in the pantry. We plant them in long rows that are three times longer than our house. It's fun to pull them up because they come up easily. We remove the greens and the dirt from them. Sometimes the dirt gets on my face and we laugh as we brush each other off before we track dirt onto Momma's floors.

Momma keeps potatoes, onions, carrots, radishes and beets in the pantry at the end of the kitchen. It is a small, dark room with no windows. It stays cooler than the rest of the house, making it a good place to store food.

To make sure we have plenty of food to eat during the cold winter months when the garden won't grow and the trees are not bearing fruit, Momma preserves fruits and vegetables in jars. It is a long process of cleaning and preparing, boiling and sealing foods in jars. I do not help with this task because I am too little,

but Yutke does. I like to watch and listen when the jars come out of the huge pot, because they pop when the lid seals. It always makes us giggle as they pop, pop, pop and Momma smiles because she knows the food is safely sealed for winter. When the jars cool, we move them to the attic for storage.

Our attic holds lots of jars of pickled vegetables from the garden and jams made from apples, pears, cherries and strawberries. The jams are Momma's favorite and she spreads them on warm bread fresh from of the oven.

Our garden needs attention nearly every day in the spring and summer to keep the weeds away and the vegetables picked as they ripen. I like to help pick cucumbers, lettuce, green beans, and tomatoes. We eat them right away, or they spoil. Cucumbers are my favorite and I sometimes eat them right in the garden. Our family loves vegetables. We have them for breakfast on our bread with butter or cheese. All of us like coffee with lots of milk in it for breakfast.

Tata owns a lot of farmland that is on the way to Grandma's house. Momma told me once that Grandma's house is six kilometers away, but it takes forever to walk there. Tata hires workers who manage part of the farm because he is at his tailor shop during the day. The workers grow lots of corn and wheat in the fields. In the spring, they plant several acres, then care for the plants until they are ready to be picked. In the fall, they harvest everything and carry it to the mill near our house. The mill grinds the corn and wheat into flour. As payment for their hard work, Tata gives part of the flour to the workers to feed their families. No money is exchanged. We use the rest of the flour to make our meals. This is how everyone has food for their families.

We also have chickens, cows, geese and ducks. The animals are easy to take care of. We throw down seeds for the chickens and they lay eggs for us every day. The cows eat grass all day in the summer months. In winter, they eat hay. Every day they give us creamy, warm milk to drink with our meals. The geese are loud and will sometimes bite. I got bitten by a goose once, then I learned how to behave around them. Momma forces corn down the geese's throats to fatten them up near harvest time. It looks so uncomfortable for the geese, so I am glad they are only force-fed for three weeks. Momma knows just how to hold the goose so it can't bite her. She says it doesn't hurt the bird and makes for a better feast. I told Momma I don't want to do that chore, so she lets me do other chores instead.

At night, our animals stay in the barn with the hay and wood that we store for the winter months. Tata and Fischel chop wood they get from the forests near our home. That is not a girl's chore because it is dangerous and requires a lot of strength. Girls prepare the food, and take care of the babies and laundry. Boys chop wood and take care of the repairs around the farm.

Momma washes clothes in the river by the mill nearly every day since she has our whole family's laundry to do. We wear our clothes several times before they get washed and we each have only a few changes of clothes.

Sometimes I help Momma carry the baskets of clothes to the river. She rubs the clothes, rinses them and wrings them out. She lets me help with rinsing and wringing. Some of the clothes are too heavy for me to wring out. When we carry them home, Momma hangs them to dry on a clothesline in our yard. In winter months, the wet sheets freeze on the line. Sometimes we throw rocks at them to soften them up. Momma doesn't like it when we throw rocks at them because the sheets might get dirty, but it really does help.

The river is a fun place to play. We swim in it during the summer months. It is always clear and cool, with the current gently tugging you down-river. We can play and splash, dive to the bottom and lazily float along the banks. In winter months, it is too cold to swim, but we still play at the edge of the river.

Sometimes we run around with our friends in the field nearby. The field is part of the ruins of a Roman castle that Momma says was built in the 1300s. The tower is still standing but the roof and most of the building are gone. No one minds that we play there. The castle grounds have the one hill where we go sledding in the winter. We like to play hide and seek and chase each other in the open area. Momma says she is glad to have some quiet at the house when we all go outdoors to play with friends.

We have lots of friends in Seredne, but no relatives live in our village. Momma and Tata's families are not too far away. We see them at simchas (celebrations) like weddings, where we get to dress up in new clothes, eat special foods, and play with our dear cousins. Our family looks forward to holiday celebrations.

I went to my cousin's Bar Mitzvah last year. When a Jewish boy turns 13, he becomes a man at his Bar Mitzvah. Fischel will have his Bar Mitzvah in a few years. Momma says, "The young man reads his brachot, which are passages from the Torah, written in Hebrew. If all goes well, they share some schnapps and say "Mazel Tov (Congratulations)!" That is it.

Tata says the Bar Mitzvah is simple, but it changes everything for a boy. He becomes a man, and may intern to learn a trade. Once he completes his internship, he begins to work.

Girls don't have a Bar Mitzvah, but they do sometimes learn a trade when they finish school, after sixth grade. Many girls become seamstresses because knowing how to sew for a family is important. Most girls marry by the time they are 18 or 20, with the help of a matchmaker. Girls plan to get married and become a mother, so learning a trade is less important for them.

Another celebration where we might see other family members happens in the fall. For seven days we have wonderful meals outdoors. Sukkot is the harvest festival where we give thanks for all the good foods we grow. Tata says it also celebrates the Bible story that tells of the survival of the Jews after 40 years in the desert. We say special prayers, but mostly this celebration is about food and eating in a specially decorated place with family.

During the Sukkot celebration, we have our meals in one of the smaller buildings on our land, called a sukkah. It has a thatched roof that is not fully closed. We always keep a table and benches in there. During the rest of the year, Momma and Tata store things in the sukkah, like wood for our stove and oven.

When the harvest comes, everything changes. We clear out the sukkah and decorate it for the celebration. We hang greenery and flowers from the thatched roof and bring out our best tablecloth and candles. Momma bakes several sweets and breads and there is more than enough food for everyone. We give thanks for the abundant harvest and our good fortune to live in a land where we can grow enough to keep our families well fed, happy, and healthy. I look forward to celebrating Sukkot with my cousins.

Even though our village isn't very big, it has nearly everything we need. When I walk down the street, many people I see are Jewish. Momma says there are about 2,000 people in Seredne and about 30 percent of them are Jewish. I can walk from one end of town to the other in 30 minutes. We don't leave the village very often because we don't need to. There are some things we buy at the general store like kerosene for our lamps, rice, bars of laundry soap, sugar and nails. If we need to see a doctor or get something important that our town doesn't have, we go to the large town on the bus that travels through once a week. Tata rode the bus to get his glasses.

Tata says the two towns around us are each a three-hour walk away. Uzhhorod is to the west and Mukacheve is to the east. He says there is only one dirt road that connects all three towns. Seredne is in the middle. In fact, the word Seredne means "middle." Our village is an important stop and we are proud to live here.

There are many shops in our village that make life on the farm easier. The cobbler makes all of Momma's shoes by hand. Momma's shoes are well-made and stylish. She keeps her shoes for many years. We children get our shoes at a store called Bata because we grow out of them so fast. Twice a year we get new shoes. When one of my older sisters grows out of her shoes, I may get her old pair.

There is also a pharmacy, a dressmaker, a fabric store, a cabinetmaker, and a pots-and-pans maker where you can either buy new pans or get your old ones repaired.

A Jewish family owns the movie house where we see live performances of traveling entertainers, or a Jewish movie. We are lucky to have a movie house since many small towns do not have one.

In the village, there is an open market where people sell their surplus items from their farms. Momma and I bring extra eggs and corn to the market. The market is a busy and lively place where most families visit. I like watching and listening to the adults as they negotiate a good trade with each other. This is how I learned to barter, which Momma lets me do sometimes. No money is exchanged. Everyone here is fair and takes home the products they need.

Our village has a mikveh (ritual bath) where Jewish people go for cleansing. I like to go with Momma to the mikveh every month. I sit to the side, watching the ladies lie on the table to have their nails clipped and their hair washed and trimmed. Momma keeps her hair short so that it will fit under the wig she wears out in public. After their tabletop care is complete, they walk over to the giant bath and climb five or six steps down into the warm water. Everyone is talking and smiling, catching up on the stories of their families and upcoming events. When I am a grown woman, I will join them at the mikveh.

Once a week, we kids get a warm bath at home, in the tin tub that Momma stores in the barn. Once Momma brings it inside and fills it with warm water, we climb in and soak. The tub is big enough for us to take baths two at a time. The warm water feels so soothing and the soap has a clean smell that stays with us well after the bath. In the summer, we sometimes bathe in the river where we swim and wash our clothes.

Another important place in our village is the post office, but it is rare to get a letter in the mail. Sometimes my mother's brother, Uncle Joseph Bohm and our Aunt Rose who live in the United States, send us packages. They send us strange-looking clothes that are so fun to show our friends and neighbors. We are very proud to have a few things from America. Tata says the post office also keeps public records, like birth certificates, on file. Tata sees the postmaster often because he orders fabric from far away places like Budapest.

Since it only takes five minutes to get to his tailor shop in the center of town, Tata walks to work every day. The shop is open six days a week with Saturdays off. Tata keeps samples of fabric and different suit designs to choose from in his shop. Several Jewish men who work for him help customers choose fabrics, then measure, cut, and sew the garments. People travel for several days to have a suit made by Tata. They say, "When Mr. Schwartz makes a suit for you, it's like he poured it on you." Momma says everyone knows Tata and respects his work. I don't think there is anything Tata is not good at.

Tata learned to sew in Budapest, where he worked as an intern, before he met Momma. He always has interns learning in his shop. Even my cousin is one of his interns.

Tata tells me that most of the Jewish men in our village are tradespeople who own the bank, the tavern, the fabric store, the shoe store, the bakery and the movie house. He says they are accomplished in our town. Many of our town's activities are arranged by the Jewish Town Council. They even choose the movies for the movie house. Most of the non-Jewish men are farmers. Tata says the Jewish businessmen are involved in the village politics because they are running the shops and bringing the products to our town.

In all families, faith is very important. Seredne has a Synagogue, a Catholic Church, and a Greek Orthodox Church. Each Saturday, men go to Synagogue in their best clothes. My Catholic friends go to their church on Sunday also in their best clothes. Their mass is in Latin, but they don't have to learn Latin, like Fischel, who studies Hebrew. In our village, people do not marry those from another faith. I know we have our own religion, but otherwise our family is just like everyone else's in the village.

Every day except Saturday, Tata gets up and has a breakfast of vegetables with bread and butter or cheese, and coffee with lots of milk in it. When he finishes eating, he walks to the Synagogue for morning prayers. The men are not there long since they all have to go to work. Next, he walks on to his shop where he begins a day of work.

We miss Tata when he is at his shop. We love when he comes home in the evening with a piece of candy in his pocket for each of us. The candy shop is next door to Tata's shop, and on the other side of his shop is the tavern. Here, travelers can stop for a meal, a drink, or even a place to sleep. Usually they continue their travels the next day. Everyone is excited to talk to newcomers and hear news. Tata always knows the latest news, even though we don't have a newspaper in Seredne. People in town talk to each other and our Rabbi. Whenever there is important news, the Rabbi is notified so he can share the information with all the families in the Synagogue.

Every Friday we prepare for Shabbat. Momma cleans and bakes more than usual. We always have chicken for dinner on Fridays. It is my job to catch the chicken, which is easy for me. Once I catch one, I take it to the butcher. Our butcher is a shochet, who is specially trained in killing and cutting meat to keep it kosher. He slices the bird's neck and hangs the bird on a metal line so the blood will drain out. When I get home with it, I pull out all the feathers so Momma can cook the special Shabbat meal. Then she sets the table in the living room with a tablecloth, candles, and freshly baked challah.

It is customary to invite strangers for dinner on Shabbat. Sometimes, Tata brings home travelers to eat with us. I like to hear their stories about faraway places.

On Friday night Momma also makes my favorite casserole, called cholent, for our Saturday meal, so she won't have to work on Saturday. It cooks overnight in the oven. Cholent is made with meat, beans and rice. When we wake up on Saturday, the meal is ready. Momma always makes extra to feed lots of people. I am happy when there is some left over for Sunday, too.

My favorite day of the week is Saturday, our day of rest. Tata goes to Synagogue every Saturday, but we only go sometimes. We have no school, no chores, and no responsibilities. We are free to play or rest all day.

Max, on the right, and his family in front of their apartment building, Cottbus, Germany, circa 1936

CHAPTER TWO

City Life in Cottbus:
Max

Our group of a dozen or so friends are all within two to three years of each other. My brother, Fred, is only one year older than me. Most of us are eight, nine, or ten years old. After school, we rush through our homework or chores so we can meet up outside to play kick ball, our favorite game. Sometimes a few of the players change, but the main group is always there.

Choosing teams is tricky because if you get on the wrong team, you will struggle to win. Fred is very good and gets chosen right away. I am not as fast as he is, so I get chosen later. Both of us are willing to fight hard to win, and do not give up easily. When we are on the same team, we know what the other person will do and can carry out plays without talking to each other.

We all get sweaty and someone usually ends up falling and scraping a knee, but we don't care. Our games are always on the right side of the street. We keep to this side of the street because we are not allowed to cross through traffic. The cement street is busy with cars and buses, and our parents worry about someone getting hurt if we cross. If our ball gets away from us and bounces across the street, the game is over for the day. That is, unless there is an adult we know who happens to be outside and notices our problem. We all yell and plead for help, and often they take pity on us and throw the ball back when traffic clears. Sometimes in the summer when people have their windows open, we holler to get someone to come out and help us. Mom knows one of the mothers who will come out to help if she hears us. She has a son about my age, so she understands how important our games are. Our best approach is just to keep the ball on our side of the street. We guard it carefully so the game can continue.

My name is Max Schindler. I was born on June 18, 1929, and I am eight years old. My family lives in Cottbus, Germany, which is south of Berlin. Dad says this is a big city with 55,000 people. We live in a multi-story apartment building that is filled with families. That is why there are so many boys to play with after school every day.

I am usually starving after playing kick ball with my friends. Mom has us wash our sweaty faces and hands in the bathroom before we come to the table for meals. Once we have washed up, she smiles and ruffles our hair, asking Fred to help set the table for dinner. My job is to clear away the dirty dishes afterward. I also take out the trash for Mom.

Mom is an excellent cook and keeps our refrigerator filled with fresh food. She likes to prepare our favorite dishes for us, helps us with homework, and tells us how we will grow to become great men. She does not work outside of the house and says we kids keep her busy at home. She loves my dad and tells him so often. She says we are lucky to have such a good life here in modern Germany.

I also have a little sister, Cecilia, who is one year younger than me. She plays with her friends in our building, but they need to stay with an adult because they are younger. Mom doesn't mind having my sister's friends over and Cecilia plays at her friends' apartments too. They like to play with dolls. They act like they are all grown up and taking care of children, which sounds boring to me. I don't want to play dolls with her.

We have a maid who helps Mom clean the house and wash the laundry. Everyone shares the laundry machines in the basement of our building. Mom asks either Fred or me to help carry the laundry up or down the stairs because there are several baskets of clothes for five people, and we live on the fifth floor.

Mom has me run down the hall to the Lowensteins' apartment to borrow an egg or a cup of flour when she unexpectedly runs out. Mom always reciprocates with something even better, something that she baked. Dad knows so many people and has friends everywhere. Sometimes he goes out to play cards with his friends, but otherwise he is home with us every night.

My parents tell us they have come a long way in life. They are both originally from Poland, and speak Polish fluently. They met, fell in love, and married in Poland. However, they wanted more than their farm life, and developed a plan to move to Germany. They speak German well, and enjoy the modern life and progressive teachings of Germany. Dad said it was important to them to move to the city before having kids, so they did just that.

Dad says Germany is known for its advanced knowledge in science, innovative ways to get information to everyone quickly, and new ways to produce things. He says Germany is the place to get the best education, so we will have the most opportunities in life.

Mom and Dad really like Germany. Once they settled in Cottbus, they had three children in three years. Fred was born in 1928, then me in 1929, and Cecilia was born in 1930. Since Fred, Cecilia and I were all born in Germany, our parents have only spoken German to us so we don't understand Polish when they speak it. When they do, it usually means there is a surprise for us.

My Dad, Benjamin, is one of nine children. He says his family is very religious, following all the Jewish laws about how to live. Therefore, he is the one who teaches us about our religion. Dad says he is pleased to see how we are growing up. He is more relaxed than his other family members about our faith and likes to say, "We are German first and Jewish second."

We do not worry about eating kosher, but we do attend synagogue regularly and try to live as good people.

My Mom, Rachela Schweid, is one of six kids. Her family is Jewish, but not as religious as Dad's family. Her family does not adhere to Jewish laws like Dad's family. Mom says that the way she lives is how she honors her faith, and she does not worry about the details of it. Together we are a good Jewish family, who attend synagogue and celebrate the Jewish holidays.

Mom says Dad had fewer business opportunities in Poland, but he found a good business in Germany. He runs a wine and liquor store. He makes enough money for us to live in our large apartment and have a maid. Our apartment is filled with new furniture with fancy carvings.

My friends and I all like Sundays. It is the only day we don't have school. On Sundays we don't do chores and Dad does not work. We sometimes take a day trip on Sunday to the mountains or the river. Mom will pack a picnic for us, or we buy food at our destination. We love swimming in the rivers and lakes that we visit.

Each Monday, we all return to school. My parents say we are getting a better education here in Germany than we could get in Poland. The Polish only go to school five days a week but we have to go Monday through Saturday. I never have any trouble with my studies. Mom is always proud of how well Fred and I complete our homework. She checks our work and ruffles our hair, saying "Good job!" when we do it correctly.

A lot of the kids in our building ride the bus to school together. I laugh and play with the other boys on the bus. Sometimes we tease the girls during our ride to school, by pulling their hair or throwing a wad of paper at them. We pretend we are innocent, and they can't tell who did it. That makes everyone laugh.

Every Friday night we attend Shabbat services at the synagogue. There aren't a lot of Jews in my neighborhood or apartment building, but there are plenty at synagogue. Mom says ours is a modern synagogue so men and women can sit together. Kids sit near the pulpit and help the Rabbi with kiddush (a prayer

said over wine). I like the way our service is filled with organ music and everyone sings, even though some people are not good singers. Mom's voice is beautiful and it fills me with warmth.

After we return home from synagogue, we celebrate Shabbat dinner by lighting candles and eating a special meal with fresh challah bread from the bakery. Dad has an easy way of helping us understand what matters, and how our faith will guide our lives. I also go to Sunday school for two hours each week where I learn more about our faith. Dad teaches Fred and me to read Hebrew in preparation for our Bar Mitzvahs.

Many of our friends go to churches in town. No one cares which faith other people practice. It seems like families only talk about their faith at home.

I always look forward to our annual summer trip to Poland. We take the train to visit my grandparents. First we stop at Grandpa Schindler's house in the small city of Brzesko. He lives alone now because Grandma Schindler passed away.

I love Grandpa and look forward to his warm hugs. His long gray beard tickles me and he knows this, so he rubs it extra on my neck just to make me laugh. He keeps special treats for us that he doesn't tell Mom or Dad about. Grandpa is very religious and tells amazing stories to help us understand our Jewish faith.

Grandpa's house is old, so we do all we can to help him fix broken windows, repair rotting floorboards and scrape old paint off the outside. When the repairs are done, we weed the garden and harvest fresh vegetables.

Our cousins come over when we visit Grandpa. I enjoy going for hikes with them in the countryside. Every time I see them, they are taller and smarter than the last time. The adults don't change much. They keep busy chatting and preparing the nice meals that we enjoy together.

Because Grandpa speaks Polish and Yiddish and we do not, we need Mom or Dad to translate his stories for us. Sometimes I can get him to tell us a funny story about Dad when he was little.

One time he told us the story of how Dad was a very busy baby. Grandma was trying to clean and chop vegetables at the table by the garden but Dad would walk away over and over again. Grandma decided to hang a clothesline between two trees where she could see him, then tied him to the clothesline with a second rope. The knot was loose enough to slide along the clothesline, allowing Dad to move freely. Dad would walk happily until he reached the end of the line, then yank and fight the rope when it pulled taut. Grandma would laugh at his frustration, then turn him around to move freely again. Dad would move along happily until he reached the limit of the rope in his new direction, when the fight would begin all over again. Grandpa chuckles and says Grandma used that rope system for quite some time after he learned to change directions when the rope pulled taut, to keep Dad safe and feeling independent. When Grandpa tells this story, his eyes twinkle and shine. He proudly remembers how Grandma came up with wise solutions to everyday problems. Dad was too small to remember the clothes line, but loves Grandpa's stories.

Grandpa's house is small for all of us, but we don't care. We love spending time with him. We usually stay here for a week, then travel on to Grandma Amalia Schweid's farm. Her home is farther into Poland and in a forest. It takes us a few days to get there by train. We play all kinds of games on the train while Dad and Mom relax. Grandpa Joseph Schweid passed away, so Grandma Amalia has a big farm to run all by herself. She works hard every day and seems happy, because she hums little songs while she is working.

Her farm is in the mountains and has a river that runs through it. We throw stones in the river, float leaves down it and poke about with fallen branches from trees. We like to swim and fish in the river too. It is cold and clean and has plenty of fish. There are endless trees to climb and play on.

Grandma Schweid is always happy to see us and wishes Mom and Dad would consider moving back here. She has a big home with plenty of room for all of us, she says. We love her playful way of getting the work done. She challenges us to see who can pick the most corn in the field, which is hard for me to win, because Fred is taller and can reach more corn. That's okay because I quickly collect the lower ears.

Each day we work the fields at Grandma's house, which

produces nearly everything we need to eat. Grandma always wants to pay us for working so hard, but we tell her we couldn't take anything from her. Instead, she takes us to her store that she runs and treats us each to a soda. I love the tingly drink, as we rarely have it at home.

Grandma's store also sells non-kosher meats, like sausages. I sometimes sneak in there and steal a sausage for myself and Fred. We don't tell Cecilia because she might not be able to keep the secret. The sausages are very tasty. I don't think Grandma minds, if she knows.

After working in the fields in the morning, we get time to play and relax in the afternoon. Climbing trees with Fred and Cecelia is one of my favorite things to do. We can hang upside down like monkeys, walk as if we are on a tight rope in the circus as we have seen in movies, hide from an imagined dangerous tiger who is stalking us, or just chase each other through the forest. It is endless fun here and so very different from our city life. We don't have to worry about traffic or crossing a busy street. We have a lot of freedom in Poland at our grandparents' houses.

Rose in a Catholic school in Seredne, after Jews could not attend public schools, circa 1938

CHAPTER THREE

Winds of Change:
Rose

Life in Seredne is changing. I don't like fourth grade as much as third grade. It is harder than last year, and other kids won't help me. So far, 1938 is not my best year. I don't understand why, but some of my friends are not talking to me as much as they used to. Some have even started ignoring me. I find myself mostly talking to my Jewish friends.

I ask Tata, "Why don't my friends like me as much as they used to? I don't know what I did wrong." Tata takes some time to think about this question before he answers.

"My little Roysie, you have done nothing wrong. In our history as Jews, there have been people who tell lies about us. Somehow, they get others to believe them. It seems there is someone working very hard to make people believe that Jews are bad right now."

25

When I frown, he makes sure to tell me again that I haven't done anything wrong.

Tata encourages me, "Just continue being the wonderful girl that you are, and everything will work out right in the end." He reminds us of the well-known Yiddish saying, "A Jew always finds a way."

This fall, we prepare the sukkah for our harvest festival as always, with beautiful greenery and flowers that hang from the branch-roof. The tablecloth is laid and candlesticks, food and drinks are set out on the table. As we all sit down for dinner, some of the neighborhood kids throw rocks at our sukkah and call us bad names. Everyone is shocked and upset by this. Tata tells us to ignore them and to continue with our celebration. He says Sukkot is a time to be gracious, happy and grateful for all our gifts. Thankfully, the neighborhood kids leave.

Within a few weeks, on the way home from school I see soldiers in the village. I have never seen soldiers before and I smile and wave at them as I walk towards our house. None of the soldiers wave back at me and suddenly I feel scared. When I get home, I ask Momma and Tata why the soldiers have come to Seredne. They tell us that the soldiers are Hungarians, and they are here to take over. Tata says there may be changes coming, but we are not to worry.

After a few weeks, I realize Tata is right. Many things are changing now with the Hungarians' arrival, and none of the changes are good. No one knows what is happening, yet no one resists. When I ask Tata why no one does anything, he says that we have to follow the rules to be good citizens. This doesn't quite make sense to me, but he explains that I will understand more when I am older.

Now the adults seem frightened when I go into the village on Fridays to get our chickens slaughtered by the shochet. In town, all the adults huddle together in small groups. I watch as they cautiously look over their shoulders before whispering together for several minutes. No one smiles and waves to me as they usually did. This puzzles me, but I figure it has something to do with the fact that everyone becomes nervous when a Hungarian soldier walks by. I also notice that people who go to our synagogue no longer talk with people that are not Jewish. I don't understand why, because until things started to change, everyone has been nice to one another. When I visit Tata at his shop, I only see Jewish customers. Tata has made suits for everyone, so it seems strange to me. Tata says not to worry about it.

Tata also says that everyone is nervous about what the change to Hungarian rule will mean for our village. Over the next few weeks, the Hungarians make many changes. The biggest change for us kids is that all Jews are not allowed to go to our public school and we must be inside our homes by 6:00 pm in the evenings. They call this a curfew. It makes me sad because I like to play outside until the sun sets and Momma calls us in for dinner.

The neighbor kids have become mean to us, throwing rocks and calling us names like "dirty Jew." They must believe the lies Tata talked about. But we have never done anything to harm anyone. The Torah says that if you do not harm others, God will not allow others to harm you. I am no longer shown respect or courtesy in any way and cannot participate in many things in our village. Hiyasura says we are now treated as second-class citizens.

One day, when I am walking and talking with Yutke, a boy calls to us from across the street, "Stop laughing and behave yourself, you dirty Jews," he yells as he picks up a rock. "I will hurt you if you don't."

Instantly we stop laughing. The look on his face is so angry that I feel tears gather in the corners of my eyes, but I will not allow myself to cry. I am a big girl and will not shame myself in the middle of town. Without saying anything, Yutke pulls me away and we head for home without completing our errand. When we get home, I sit by the fire alone while Yutke quietly tells Momma what happened.

Later, when I talk to Tata about it, he hugs me. I tell him that I think it is best to just be quiet, and Tata agrees. It is scary to be around non-Jews because we don't know if they are our friends any more. Tata tells us everything will be okay, but we need to be patient. Things are changing quickly and there is so much that I don't understand. I try not to worry because Tata says we will be fine.

Tata tells us that we will now attend a Catholic school run by nuns. He says the nuns are concerned when any child is held out of school, and agreed to add Jewish children into their classes. They dress differently than the teachers I know, but teach us in much the same way. They talk about the Catholic religion a lot and when they do, we are excused to play on the playground. Our public school did not talk about religion at all, so this is different for me. I don't mind the Catholic school; in fact, the extra time on the playground is fine with me.

On the last day of the school year, Sister Mary approaches me as I am getting ready to leave. "Roysie, I must speak with you," she tells me quietly.

"Yes, Sister?" I am worried that she will slap my wrists for not doing well on my math lesson yesterday. I've always hated math and yesterday's lesson was especially hard.

"Roysie, today will be your last day at school."

I am puzzled by this statement and look at her for a moment.

"Yes, Sister. I will see you in a few weeks when school starts again," I say, wondering why she is telling me this.

"No, Roysie. Fourth grade is your last year with us. You will not be allowed back here. Jews will not be allowed to attend this school any longer," the nun says. Her face looks sad. I feel my face flush, but I refuse to show any emotion.

"I understand. Thank you, Sister," I say. I quickly gather my things and leave the classroom.

As I walk home with my sisters that day, I feel the burn of shame in my face, but I also feel relieved. When I tell Momma what the sister said, she shakes her head but says nothing. Momma has plenty for us to do at home to run the farm and household, so I will not miss school.

It is September 1939, and I am nearly ten years old. I don't like the new Hungarian rules, but we are doing fine staying at home with Momma. I don't miss going to school at all.

Tonight, Tata has a strange look on his face when he walks in the house. He looks pale and is pacing back and forth. He seems to be having trouble saying what he means, then tells Momma that his shop and everything in it is gone.

"Gone? What do you mean?" Momma asks, her eyes getting big. I can see her hands start to shake as she suddenly sits down heavily on one of the kitchen chairs.

"I was cutting fabric for Mikael Rosenberg's Bar Mitzvah suit when three Hungarian soldiers walked into the shop. They approached me and told me that all of us have to leave. They said that all Jewish businesses now belong to them and that we were to leave and never return." Tata's voice shakes. He, too, sits down on a chair, running his hand through his hair.

"Solomon, what are we to do?" Momma asks quietly, almost to herself. After a moment of silence, she looks up at Tata and then at me. As if she has just realized that we can hear her, she shoos all of us out of the kitchen so that she and Tata can talk alone.

A little while later, I hear Hiyasura and Yutke talking about what we will do now that Tata's job and all our money have been taken away. When Yutke spies me listening, she quickly shushes Hiyasura and they busy themselves cleaning. I do not understand everything that is happening, or why they don't want me to know about it.

Thankfully, Tata has one sewing machine and some fabrics with him. Though he cannot work in the shop, he can work at home. All of the Jewish store owners have the same problem. The tavern, the bank, the bakery, the cobbler, the fabric store and the movie house are all in the hands of the Hungarians now, who have given them to non-Jews. The whole town changed today.

I cannot understand why Tata is not angrier about his store being taken away from him. I want to yell at the Hungarians. Tata tells me that would be very dangerous and we are fine without the store. He says he will just sew from home. Adults are strange to me. Their rules don't make sense. I thought we were not allowed to steal from others. It surely seems to me like the Hungarians are stealing Tata's store.

Momma and Tata try to keep life as normal as possible with the Hungarians now in charge, but nothing is the same. There are limits on nearly everything we do. We only eat food that we have grown on our farm, and I long for things like the candy Tata used to bring home for us. Everyone knows not to ask Tata or Momma for things because there is no way they can give them to us. Life is not normal at all and news has spread that Germany is at war with Poland. No one knows what will come next.

Max's paternal grandfather, Simon Schindler's house in Brzesco, Poland, circa 1923

CHAPTER FOUR

Deported to Poland:
Max

It is the fall of 1937 now, and after just a few weeks back at home from a relaxing summer at Grandma Schweid's farm, I realize that something is very different. It's not just nerves about returning to school. The adults are whispering in grocery store lines, while washing laundry in the basement, and at Dad's store. Even Mom and Dad wait for us to leave the room to talk. Something is just not right. I know Fred senses it as well, so we ask Mom and Dad what is going on.

They are slow to respond and speak to each other in Polish for a few minutes, which feels like an hour to me. Finally, they turn to the two of us and say, "We need to be sure your sister is asleep, because she is too young to hear this conversation."

We wait until she goes to bed and falls asleep. It feels like a week, and when we finally continue, Fred and I are worried.

Mom and Dad sit us down and tell us they want to be honest with us, but will need us to be very adult-like in handling what they are about to say. They explain there are rumblings about trouble to come. Dad says, "This is the reason we have been talking in Polish more often lately and listening to the radio in the evenings."

It seems there is a growing concern about Adolf Hitler who has a hatred for all Jews, and that there is a possibility of war. Dad says he knows all these topics are troublesome, and he hopes to get us out of Germany. He is in contact with our relatives in the USA who will help us get the papers needed to emigrate there. I can't imagine moving all the way to the United States. It scares me to think we have to leave Cottbus and move so far away.

As the fall months wear on in 1937, Dad says the situation for Jews in Germany is changing steadily. It seems that Hitler is gaining popularity and his power is increasing. He is circulating propaganda in the newspapers, on the radio and in the movies to make people hate Jews. Dad is concerned about Fred and me because there is growing aggression toward Jews in public. We reassure Dad that we are not suffering at school, which makes him feel a little better.

One day, Dad comes home from work to tell us there are yellow Jewish stars and signs painted on the windows of his store that say "Juden Raus" meaning "Jews get out of here." Mom is genuinely frightened that something bad might happen to Dad at work. He assures her that all will be fine, but we must be careful when we are out in public. Mom, Fred and I promise Dad that we will always stay alert and be careful.

A few days later, Dad comes home from work looking pale and tired. Mom can see that something is wrong, so she sends us to our room. We know there is a big problem and listen carefully at their door to hear what they are saying but cannot make out their conversation.

Finally, we hear Mom shout, "But Benjamin, how will we survive?"

I can tell Mom is shocked and frightened about what Dad just told her, but they do not say anything at all to us tonight. Fred and I talk after Cecilia goes to bed. It must be bad because Mom and Dad always tell us what is happening. It is difficult to fall asleep with all the possibilities running through my mind.

The next day, Dad informs us that the Germans came to his liquor store and took all its contents. He was ordered not to return. Fred and I jump up yelling, "They can't do that!"

He orders us to sit down and listen. He continues, saying that throughout the ordeal people were throwing rocks and calling him a dirty Jew. He had no choice but to walk away.

Dad wants us to understand that we are in no position to resist the Germans. Doing so could have serious consequences. He will now become a traveling liquor salesman. This means he will be away from us for days at a time, and he needs to know that we will be careful.

"Do not go outdoors alone," he says. We assure him that we understand and will be very careful. Fred and I will stay together and watch out for Cecilia and Mom while he is away.

At synagogue, we overhear the Rabbi speaking quietly to a group of adults, "The Germans walked in and put a gun to his head. They took Schindler's store, bank account, means of income and integrity all in one act."

We know this is true even though Dad did not tell us everything, because the Rabbi would never lie.

"We have to get out of here as soon as possible," Dad frets.

Dad continues to try to move the paperwork along for emigration to the U.S., but there is no resolution yet. Since he still has a family to feed, he works very hard at traveling sales to support us.

Mom tries to keep our lives as normal as possible at home. She never complains, even though Dad is gone during the weekdays. Sometimes her eyes are red and swollen in the mornings as she fixes breakfast, but she doesn't talk about why. Dad always comes home by Friday night so that we can go to synagogue and have Shabbat dinner together. Mom makes sure to prepare a pleasing Shabbat meal for all of us, but especially for Dad who sometimes

33

looks so tired. We know life is much harder for him.

Dad tells us he lives with anti-Semitism daily now. He is not able to be with us every day and tells us he is worried about what will happen in his absence. He warns us to avoid conflict at all costs, stay quiet and follow the orders of officers. We assure Dad that we are not suffering. The world is difficult to navigate as a Jew now, and we know Dad's concerns are legitimate.

Dad is more eager than ever to get us out of Germany. He has completed the paperwork for the entire family to move to the United States with the help of his relatives in San Francisco, California. Even with their help, there are many hurdles to jump. The papers take longer than Dad thinks they should, so he is anxious, although there is nothing more he can do to speed up the process. Dad frowns when he talks about it, but he assures us we will be fine.

While we await authorization to emigrate, Mom and Dad take classes to learn new skills so they can work when we get to the United States. I overheard Mom tell our neighbor that she and Dad chose to learn the laundry business, on the advice of their cousins in San Francisco, who say Chinese immigrants are very successful in making a life in the laundry business there.

In September of 1938, after another fun summer in Poland, we again prepare to return to school. This year I will be in fourth grade. Fred is entering fifth grade and will go to a new school, a junior high school. I can tell he is nervous about the change, as he is shy and it takes him a while to get to know new people.

Fred's new school is called Adolf Hitler Junior High School. He gains admission because he is considered a foreigner (from Polish parents) and is therefore protected. If he were a local German Jew, he would not be admitted. International rules protect the Polish people in Germany. Mom advises Fred to pretend he is comfortable. I wish I could help him, but this time he must figure it out for himself.

From the very beginning, Fred is treated poorly at his new school and feels like an outsider. The other students do not like him and don't include him, because he is Jewish. He is ignored. Fred does not complain at school or at home, but I can see he is struggling. The two of us only talk about how bad his school is when we are alone. I repeat the things Dad has taught us about managing ourselves in an aggressive environment. Dad has been suffering this kind of treatment for two years by now, but he is an adult who knows how to cope. It is so hard for me to see my brother suffer and not be able to do anything to help him. He feels very alone at school.

Fred's personality is quiet, so I hope that will keep him from being noticed. He says he keeps his mouth shut and avoids other students. He just hopes we will leave Germany soon. Meanwhile, my school and my friends treat me like they always have, and this makes Fred's situation even harder for him.

On October 28, 1938, I am nine years old and settling into fourth grade math class where we are working on the eight times-tables. Although it is not common, on this day I make an error in multiplying. My teacher approaches me and slaps me across the face. I am shocked. It's not the pain from the slap that upsets me. I am upset because no one has ever treated me like this at school before, and I don't know how to respond. For the moment, I choose to be quiet so as not to draw attention to myself again. I will have to think about what is happening here before I choose to act. My cheek burns from the slap and from shame.

Later that day, two German SA officers known as Storm Troopers or Brownshirts come into the class and call out my name. I stand at my desk to acknowledge that they called me, wondering why. Did they somehow know about the math error for which I'd been slapped? My heart is pumping even harder than it was after the slap. The officers approach me, take me under the arms and begin walking. I have no idea where we are going or why, and I have no choice but to go with them. I don't understand what is happening. The German SA officers don't explain anything and I decide not to ask, despite being very frightened and wanting to know where they are taking me. They march me out of the school and through town, never pausing or explaining what is happening. Along the way, we pass our synagogue where people ask, "Where are you going?" I respond that I don't know.

We march straight to the local jail and they shove me behind bars without any explanation. The jail is loud, confusing, and frightening. There are many other Polish Jews with me in jail. I can tell by their clothes that all of them were taken from their task at hand and brought directly here. There are women who are still in their aprons from cooking in their kitchens, men are wearing suits from their work, children have their schoolbags from their classroom. No one understands what is happening. Many keep asking for explanations and some are crying. Jews of all ages and professions have been rounded up and brought to this jail.

I remain quiet so I might hear what is happening to all of us. I remember Dad's advice not to draw attention to myself. I am so frightened. I review my day. No child should be slapped for making a math mistake, then dragged to jail. As I am trying to remain calm in this room filled with uncertainty, I see others my age crying or screaming.

Suddenly, the door opens, and they shove in a new group of Jews. I rapidly inspect every face that crosses the threshold. When my eyes meet Mom's, she bursts out crying. She quickly tries to compose herself as she and Dad make their way over to me. Both Dad and I have quiet tears. Hugging them, I see Cecilia and Fred. I have never been so relieved as I am now, standing together again as a family. I worry about my parents' reaction. Will they be angry with me for getting arrested?

"Max, we are so happy to see you," Fred says. "We didn't know if we would ever see you again!"

"Why?" I ask as I feel my eyebrows rising.

"You will never believe what happened at home today," Fred says. "Dad had just arrived home from work and Mom was beginning to cook dinner when two SA officers stopped at our home and demanded we all come with them. Dad refused to leave without you, Max, as he knew you would return home from school soon. The officers allowed us to wait thirty minutes for you during which time Dad and Mom packed three suitcases of belongings to take with them. Mom packed food and clothes while Dad packed things he thought might be of value if we got into trouble. Everyone was nervous and scared since the SA officers would not tell us where we were going, so I snuck into our parent's room and quietly asked Dad questions as he packed. Dad explained that he was packing these things because he wanted to be able to trade with others to get items we might need to escape if possible. He brought jewelry, money, the expensive desk set, and anything else he thought might be worth something. The officers became impatient and interrupted our packing to take us away. Mom and Dad were beside themselves with worry for you."

SA officers marched my family to the jail. Fred said he had never seen that stricken look on Mom and Dad's faces before. It was truly frightening.

While I reflect on everything Fred just told me, the officers command everyone to listen up. "All Polish Jews are being sent back to Poland."

Dad says they call it the repatriation of Jews to Poland, but he says the truth is Polish Jews are now exiled from Germany. He tells us not to ask him or anyone else any questions, just do what we are told. He will explain all he can when we are in a safe location. Dad reminds us to be grateful that at least we are together as we are forcibly being removed from Germany.

Shortly thereafter, everyone in the jail is told to march in a group. The SA guards lead the march to the nearby train station and keep a careful watch on all of us. We each make our way to a table staffed by Germans where we must give our names, ages and addresses. The information is recorded in a book, then they make us move along until we are forced to get on a train car. As I climb onto the train, I realize it is packed with Polish Jews. There is no extra room at all. The doors are then locked. Dad says the train is moving toward Poland.

German SA officers make their way through the train cars and search the passengers for money. They tell everyone there is a directive sent down that Jews can only have 50 Marks in their possession. If someone has more than that, the officers confiscate the money. Dad has to hand over almost all of our money as well. No one resists this injustice, but our parents' faces show me how much of a problem this is for our family. Mom and Dad are speaking in Polish to each other again.

The train makes many stops along the way, picking up more people and packing them into some of the other train cars. There is no more room in our car. After several hours, the train comes to a halt. All is quiet initially, then a burst of activity begins as the soldiers unlatch the engine from the cars we are in, so it can return to Germany. It takes some time, but we can feel and hear the movement of the engine on the tracks as it leaves us behind. The guards unlock our train car and allow everyone to leave. Mom and Dad tell us they saw a sign as we pulled into the station, and that we are in Zbaszyn, Poland.

Mom and Dad feel certain it isn't safe to remain here. They inform us that we have an uncle who lives nearby who they need to contact. They tell the three of us kids, "Do not move. Stay where you are on the train, while we go and make arrangements for the rest of our trip. We need more money to buy train tickets. Your uncle will help us."

We three share a look and nod to confirm the plan as we hold hands. Mom and Dad then get off the train and we are alone. There are many people all around us, but I feel so afraid. We try to reassure each other that it will all be fine. The wait feels like hours, when all of a sudden, the train gives an unexpected jolt and begins moving. My eyes grow wide and my heart pounds so loudly that I am sure others can hear it. I want to scream. I look at Fred for guidance but when I make eye contact with him, I realize he is just as frightened as I am and neither of us knows what to do. Fred and I frantically agree that we cannot separate from Mom and Dad. We make a split-second decision to shove our suitcases out the train window and jump off the train.

We begin moving as quickly as possible, making sure Cecilia is with us. It is tremendously scary to jump through the window, but even worse would be to lose Mom and Dad. The train has not gained much speed yet, so the fall should be manageable.

"No time to waste," I call out.

I indicate where each of us should go and we line up at three windows in a row.

"On the count of three we all jump at the same time. Ready, one, two, three!"

We land hard on the ground, near each other. I can see Fred and Cecilia on either side of me and take a deep breath of relief. I stand up and brush off the dirt, and realize I am fine. Cecilia is crying but doesn't seem to be hurt too badly. It's just her wrist, she says as she rubs it. I help her gather her bag and we check on Fred. He too is fine and brushing off dirt. We are together and safe, and my heart can begin to calm down now. I thought it might pop out of my chest. My heart has done things today that it has never done before. As I look down at Cecilia, I realize she needs to be comforted. I wrap my arms around her and reassure her that she was brave and we will be fine when Dad and Mom return.

After what seems like an eternity, Mom and Dad come back and find us sitting beside the railroad tracks. They rush forward asking what happened, why are we off the train? Their faces cannot hide their fear. It has been a terrible day and this is just one more potentially dangerous situation. We try to explain that the train began moving and we feared being separated from them. Both Mom and Dad reassure us that we did the right thing by choosing to try to stay together. It is not possible for any of us to know exactly what is happening and how to cope. Our family quickly boards the train that now has a new engine and will take us farther into Poland. Dad explains that the movement of the train likely happened when the new engine was attached. Now that the train is moving forward, Mom and Dad calmly remind us how important it is to stay together and follow their directions, no matter what. There is so much happening and everything changes so quickly, which makes it dangerous. They will try to keep one parent with us at all times now, as we start a new life today.

Dad learned of a Jewish organization that assists families to unite with local Jewish families in Poland. He made arrangements for us to stay with a family in Poznan. At the train station, there is food for all of us. I had not realized how hungry I was until I smelled the warm bread. When we finish eating, we are led by a local man to a nearby home. He mentions that we will stay as guests of the Jewish community. The family is kind, and gives us a place to sleep overnight. Dad waits for money to be wired to him, so he can buy train tickets to go further into Poland, which takes a few days. It is fun to meet new friends and play together, but Mom

and Dad still look very nervous.

When the next train becomes available, we take it to Katowice, Poland where we stay for two weeks with Uncle Solomon Schweid and Aunt Helena. They have a nice home and plenty of food which they happily share with us. It is a great relief to be with people we know and are comfortable with rather than strangers, after being taken from our home. Our parents look more relaxed now and are making plans with my aunt and uncle. My uncle owns a jewelry store, and my aunt recently had a baby. We love our little cousin and play together during our stay at their home.

In the middle of November, 1938, our parents decide to continue on to Brzesko, Poland, to Grandpa Schindler's house. We will stay in his little old house with the metal roof. It will be like we are camping. Mom and Dad continue to try to figure out a better solution for us, though.

Because Grandpa's old house is sinking, the windows are low enough that they are near the ground. We enjoy climbing into the house through one window and running through the house to climb outside again through another window. Grandpa doesn't mind us running through his house, which Mom would never allow us to do before.

After two weeks, our parents tell us we are leaving. This time, we head to Grandma Schweid's home in Wytrzyszczka, Poland. Her big farmhouse has enough space for all of us. Also, because the farm is in a small village out in the country, there seems to be less risk of German soldiers finding us. Mom and Dad let us know that this is where we plan to stay.

When we are off by ourselves, I admit to Fred that I feel a bit out of place here in the country, because I'm a city kid. Grandma's farm is self-sustaining with horses, cows, ducks and chickens, fields with crops, and a big garden. I am not accustomed to this much farming, caring for animals, using an outhouse, and lighting kerosene lamps instead of turning on a switch. Fred feels the same, but we both know not to complain. This is our new life, and we need to adjust because there are no other options. We get lessons in all farm-life topics because we must work the farm to help our family. Dad cannot sell liquor like he did before. He is now a farmer. I only talk to Fred about how different it is not to have electricity or indoor plumbing, movie houses, or bicycles. We both agree that farm life offers a lot of outdoor freedoms that we enjoy. We know the plan is to stay here, so we do our best to cope with the changes. When I feel unhappy, I climb one of my favorite trees and pretend I'm a monkey.

Dad, Fred, and I work in the fields where we grow potatoes, beets and wheat. Dad also does a little bit of trading in town with Polish merchants, to purchase items we cannot produce on the farm, like kerosene, salt and sugar. He sells our clothes and the things he brought from Germany in the three suitcases to secure the needed items. Mom works hard with the women to care for the animals, the garden, do the laundry and cook the meals. Mom and Dad try very hard to make our life stable and easy for us, despite all the changes.

While we are working in the fields hoeing, picking or planting, Dad teaches us about farming and our Jewish faith. I am learning to appreciate living off the land and adjusting to this new country lifestyle. There is comfort in the repetitive nature of farming. At least we know what each day will be like.

Our parents enroll the three of us in public school, where everyone speaks Polish. School is more challenging because I don't understand the language, but because our parents are native Polish speakers, they help us develop language skills at home. They can also read our schoolbooks to us and help us with our homework. The Polish kids are not kind to us, or any of the Jewish children. The Jewish students stick together and avoid the Polish kids as much as possible. We only have to go to school five days a week instead of six days a week, like we did in Germany.

I notice the customs here are different than in Germany. If you pass a teacher on a country road, you take off your cap and lower your head. I have never seen this before in my city, but quickly try to pick up the customs of my new home so I can blend in. I do not want to draw attention to myself. I learn to speak Polish as quickly as I can. Non-Jewish Polish people and their children are anti-Semitic, making my efforts to blend in extremely difficult.

In 1939, Grandma Schweid predicts that war is inevitable.

The Schindlers and Schweids know war is coming and this is very serious for all Jews. As a result, our other family members from Mom's side move into Grandma Schweid's big house as well. Each family takes one room. Five families totaling ten kids now live in Grandma Schweid's house. We are all trying to escape the horrors of war, and work together to run the farm. Grandma Schweid is happy to have all her family with her.

I am thrilled to have extended family live with us. We know and trust them as Jews and as family. My cousins understand the challenges at school and have the same fears I do. Because there is hostility and prejudice toward Jews, my cousins, Fred, Cecilia and I go to school together in one large group. That way, we are less likely to get picked on.

As the war approaches, the hostility and aggression toward Jews gets noticeably worse. My Polish classmates harass me and want to fight with me. I get involved in some serious fights with these kids. Our fights often include throwing rocks into homes. The situation has become truly dangerous. I am fortunate to have my brother and cousins close by because when kids attempt to fight with me, I can always find support in my family members. We usually have five boys ready to counter any potential aggressors. Together, we can outdo the smaller groups that fight us. In this way, other kids learn over time to leave us alone. They give my family a wide berth and go around us, rather than try to challenge us.

Dad learns through relatives who remain in Germany that our apartment and belongings are still intact. Somehow, those relatives were not exiled. Dad arranges to ship our furniture and belongings from our apartment to Brzesko. When it arrives by train, he rents a couple of rooms in a house to store it for later use, near Grandpa Schindler's home.

While living on the farm, we continue practicing our faith and its teachings. We follow our religious traditions in the village Shtiebel (small house of prayer) since there is no synagogue. After Friday services, we have Shabbat dinner and rest or read. Dad reads the Hebrew prayers, which I cannot yet read. He still teaches Hebrew to Fred and me, so we can one day have our Bar Mitzvahs.

In late 1939, Grandma Schweid's prediction comes true and war breaks out with Germany. My parents are very worried about our safety and don't know what to do, because our immigration papers have not arrived. Finally, they decide we need to leave the village. We travel back to Brzesko on the train, to Grandpa Schindler's home, thinking the small city has better access to amenities and transport than the little village of Wytrzyszczka. Within a day or two of the beginning of the war, the Poles align with the Germans. They put on German uniforms and want to be part of the German war effort. They call themselves the Polish Fox Deutsche, and circulate rumors that the whole city of Brzesko is going to be gassed. The local people are very frightened and go indoors, sealing their windows with tape to keep the gas out. All the villagers, including us, stay inside for two or three days. As a result, the streets are barren of people. This is how the Germans march in to take over the city of Brzesko without firing a single shot.

The Germans now occupy all of Poland and have taken over. There is a real possibility of being captured during the German SS roundups. The Jews that are caught are sent to a ghetto or a concentration camp. My parents are frantic about this possibility and will do nearly anything to avoid it. They have heard about the horrors of life in the ghettos and concentration camps. In the end, they decide to take the family back to Grandma Schweid's village again, to evade the horrible alternatives. They believe that staying in the rural part of Poland is now the safest place for our family. Dad says no one could have predicted that German soldiers would come into Brzesko and take over without any resistance.

Our parents are frightened and trying to find a safe place for us, I know. I am terrified. There doesn't seem to be any good choices left. Dad likes to have a plan and the war interferes with every plan he makes. After gathering whatever is useful from our stored goods in Brzesko, we again take the train back to Wytrzyszczka and Grandma Schweid's home. This time we plan to remain on the farm while the Germans are in Poland.

So many things keep changing while we are in occupied Poland. The German officers nail orders to trees and signs-posts to communicate the latest edicts. This is how we learn that Jewish kids can no longer attend school.

I do not miss going to school, but think about my parents stressing how important my education is. With no classes in the village, we remain on the farm caring for the fields, gardens and animals. We rarely see any non-Jewish neighbors. I'm fine with that since we avoided interactions with them before. Now they completely ignore us, except when they try to start a fight. We try to be invisible to avoid issues.

Another edict is posted in 1941, ordering all Jews to wear a Jewish star on their clothes, over their heart. Mom sews the stars on our clothes for us while explaining that we must follow the orders to avoid being punished. We know that many have lost their lives by resisting. The Germans are dangerous and unpredictable, so we do what we are told.

Many times, the Germans march down the main street, near Grandma's house. When this happens, news of the German soldiers coming travels quickly to families. This time, we hear about them from the neighbors and move hurriedly and quietly into the forest to hide. Mom grabs food and water because we may stay all day long, or even overnight, until the Germans leave the area. While we are hiding in the woods, Grandma stays in her store and acts relaxed and normal serving the German soldiers, to keep us safe. She tells them she is an old widow just trying to make a living. The soldiers must believe her because they do not search for us. Mom and Dad talk about how brave she is. Grandma is risking her life because if the soldiers found out she was hiding Jews on her farm, we would all certainly be shot.

Auschwitz II-Birkenau Concentration Camp, Poland

CHAPTER FIVE

Childhood Stripped Away:
Rose

In 1941, I am nearly 11 years old and there is another new rule in Seredne. We must wear a gold Star of David on our sleeves so everyone will know we are Jewish. I don't understand why only Jewish people have to wear an identifying patch and follow special rules. Maybe it has to do with the fact that Hungarians don't like Jewish people. Aunt Lea and I discuss this as she sews the yellow stars onto my sleeves. I ask her why I often hear non-Jewish people talking about bad things Jews have done. She says she doesn't know any Jews that have done bad things and I shouldn't worry about what other people say.

"What other people say and think is none of our business." Aunt Lea says.

A few months later, another change comes to our family. On Sunday, the men and boys that are old enough are rounded up by soldiers and loaded onto trucks. This includes Tata and Fischel. They are driven out of town and as I watch the truck pull out of sight I wonder where they are taking them. A few days later, when the men haven't returned, I hear women in the village questioning aloud to one another if the men are ever coming back. Tata will find a way to come home to us, I know.

When the men finally arrive home on a Friday night, Tata and Fischel look exhausted as they descend from the truck. Tata's face has deep grooves in it that are dark brown with dirt. Fischel's clothes, which used to be blue and grey are now a muddy brown. Flakes of caked-on mud shed off of his clothes as he makes his way over to us. When they approach, they say nothing, only nod at us tiredly. Tata smiles at me when I wave and takes my hand in his as we walk toward the house.

Later that night, after Tata and Fischel wash up and we are all sitting around the Shabbat dinner table, Tata tells Momma that they are being forced to work for the Germans. It is hard labor and the men feel like slaves, as they are never paid for their work. They are given little food and little water. When Momma asks what they are doing for the Germans, Tata says they pave roads, cut wood for bridges, lay foundations, dig ditches and sometimes they work in factories. No matter what they are doing, they work hard, long hours. The guards watch them closely throughout the day, and threaten anyone who isn't working hard enough. Tata says he and Fischel keep their heads down and work steadily so they can come home to us on Friday nights.

On Sunday morning Tata and Fischel are forced back onto the truck and taken away again. This happens again and again as weeks and months go by. Momma tries to put on a brave face for us kids, but I know she misses Tata and is worried about him and Fischel. I miss Tata terribly. I miss the conversations during meals and I even miss Fischel's complaints about food, because he is such a fussy eater.

One night when Tata and Fischel are sitting quietly by the stove, I ask Tata why no one does anything about this situation.

For what feels like years now, we have people taking things from us and demanding we do what they say. The men work for the Germans under Hungarian supervision, and are away from their families six days a week. Are they not angry that they are being forced to work like slaves without pay?

Tata sighs and says, "Roysie, we have to be patient and follow the rules since we are not in charge. Of course we would like to be paid, but we can't force them to pay us. God will reward us for being kind to the Hungarians." At 13 years old, the ways of the world are more perplexing to me than they were when I was younger. I lean on Tata to explain things to me. Maybe it is because I have not been able to go to school for five years that I just don't understand.

A few weeks later, I am on my way to the shochet to have him butcher the chicken I caught for Shabbat when I overhear the village crier beating on his drum to get people's attention. I walk quickly toward the center of the village to hear what he has to say. People whisper all around me that Jews are to turn in their radios. We are no longer allowed access to public information or news programs. I hear whispers among the adults about what could be happening in other places. Many people look grim and shake their heads as they head home to inform their families.

I run nearly all the way home to tell Momma. I learn later that only one Jewish family keeps a radio in the cellar of their home, defying the rule. This is a huge risk because if the Hungarians find out, they will kill all the people in the house. Momma is very stern with us that we are not to tell anyone about the radio. We will not be responsible for the death of our neighbors. The neighbors listen at night and whisper to others of what is happening outside our village. Children are not allowed to listen, so I only hear information by eavesdropping on Momma's conversations with Aunt Lea as they work in the kitchen.

On Friday night, Tata says our Rabbi told the congregation that they must comply with this demand from the Hungarians, and not to resist, for resistance is not the work of God. So many things are taken from us, but not our religion. It is comforting to have our faith. We continue to worship and attend Synagogue, where the Rabbi shares any news he hears. At Synagogue, we feel safe surrounded by people who think like us, understand our ways, and know the same struggles. We are all feeling like prisoners in our own town.

We cannot leave Seredne without approval from an officer in charge. When I ask Momma why, she says that the Hungarians want to track where the Jews are going. I wonder about this for a while and later, I hear Hiyasura say that they just want to prevent us Jews from interacting with non-Jews. Talking to non-Jewish people these days isn't very pleasant, so it doesn't bother me much.

The real problem comes if a Jew needs to see a doctor. Even if they have something seriously wrong, they have to get permission from the Hungarians to go. I don't understand why they would want to stop people from seeing a doctor. Don't they know that without a doctor, people could die? When I ask Momma and Tata about this, they tell us everything is going to work out and we should not worry. They remind us that God will protect us from harm. They repeat this to us many times, and I sometimes wonder if they tell it to themselves even when we aren't around. One night I hear Hiyasura and Yutke talking about it after they think I've gone to sleep.

"Do you think things will ever go back to the way they were before?" Yutke whispers as they speak into the darkness.

"I don't think so," Hiyasura answers. "Things are harder for Jews now. Tata has no income and Momma needs our help even more in trying to keep the house and farm running smoothly. We can't buy things we don't grow or make anymore, so we settle for what we have."

"I miss our cousins and new clothes," Yutke laments.

"I miss books, chocolate, and the smell of new paper," Hiyasura replies.

They talk a little while longer, but I am sleepy so I don't hear any more of their conversation.

In the morning, I wake up to caring for the house, working in our garden, and living our life as best we can with Momma. Thankfully, we have enough to eat from the farm and our animals since there is less extra for us to trade in the market now. The items we are trading for, such as sugar and salt, are essential.

In the spring of 1944, I am nearly 14 years old and living under the fascist rule of the Hungarians. My Seredne is different, locked down under their rule. Jews are prisoners in our village, forced to stay put and avoid being seen or noticed. Non-Jews run the town, having taken over all the shops. Momma looks tired and Tata is gone most of the time. I miss him so much, especially because he always helped me understand the world. Right now, the world doesn't make any sense to me. I miss my old life, even school.

One morning, a month before Passover, as I am playing with my sisters in the lane, I hear loud noises coming from down the road. As we watch, soldiers in dark green uniforms and black helmets march into town. They wear tall black boots, thick leather belts with shiny belt buckles, and a large red armband with a spider on it. I am unsure who these soldiers are. I have never seen uniforms like these before. This time I do not wave to the soldiers. They make me feel worried.

I wander closer to town after sending my little sisters home, to try to learn what new rules these soldiers will impose on our already limited routine. When I get to the edge of town, I see adults whispering in small groups.

"Germans," I hear several women whisper. I study the outfits of the soldiers as I wonder how these women know them to be German. Have they come to take over our country?

I creep my way along from one block to the next as I watch these newcomers gather in the square. I linger behind several villagers to listen and learn what I can.

"Those are the SS," one announces.

"What is the SS?" another asks.

"The Secret Service. I heard they are the most brutal of the German Nazi forces."

"Maybe now they will finally rid us of our dirty Jewish problem," the first woman leers as the others nod and walk away. I duck behind a building so they will not see me. I know if they see the yellow star on my jacket sleeve, they will call me names or even hit me.

I am not sure what this means for us, but I can tell by the looks on the faces of the Jewish adults nearby that this is not good. It is getting close to six o'clock, our curfew time, so I make my way home as I think about this new development. When I arrive, I tell Momma what I saw and heard, but she just nods and shakes her head. I don't dare ask what she is thinking or try to imagine what might come next.

We continue to do chores, play in the field and help Momma in the house. She makes sure that everything goes on as it always has, baking, cleaning, and teaching me how to sew.

One day, as we are all chopping vegetables in the kitchen, Momma interrupts the conversation with a very serious look on her face.

"Girls, I know that things are confusing. You need to continue to act as if nothing is wrong. Acting strangely can get us into trouble. If you mind your own business and act natural, the soldiers will ignore you and leave you alone."

Hiyasura and Yutke nod. I nod along with them, although I don't understand what she means. When I ask Hiyasura about it later, she tells me not to worry and let Momma handle it. I try not to think about it, as I trust that Momma and Tata will keep us safe and not let anything bad happen to us.

A few weeks go by and we prepare for Passover. I am excited to sit around the dinner table with my family and eat special food. So often lately we are not all at home together. On the first night of Passover, we gather around the table and say our prayers before we eat. Tata prays a little extra long this year, but I don't mind because he and Fischel are with us tonight.

Fischel does not complain once about the food and even seems happy with all the choices. He looks thinner than usual today, but he has a smile on his face. We all enjoy sitting together around the finely set table, eating and talking. Tata makes jokes and all of us kids laugh loudly, while Momma watches and smiles. It almost feels like old times, when we didn't have so many restrictions.

When the seven days of Passover are over, Momma sends me to the bakery to buy bread. During Passover, we eat no bread. I cannot wait to taste bread again and hurry to town to buy it. On my way out of the bakery, with my fresh loaves tucked under my arm, I hear the town crier beating his drum. I join the other people and gather around him to listen to his news. He tells everyone that all Jews are being shipped out by train. They need to pack a bag of belongings and go to the school within 48 hours. I rush home to tell Momma, but she has already heard the news. I am relieved Tata and Fischel are home and not at work camp so we can all be together.

Momma and Tata also know we need to bring valuables to the school for registration and safe keeping. Tata decides not to follow this rule and wants to hide our valuable jewelry instead. He asks the three older girls to come with him to see where he plans to stash our family valuables. Hiyasura and Yutke do not want to know the hiding place, so I am the only one who watches Tata put our jewelry in a shoe polish box. He leads me to a dark corner of the house and motions for me to pull a chair over. Tata climbs up onto the chair and places the box on a crossbeam near the ceiling. Stepping off the chair, Tata grabs a bucket and goes outside to fill it with mud. I follow him back into the house and watch as he covers the shoebox with mud so no one can tell there is anything hidden there at all. I assure Tata that I will never forget the jewelry, so we can recover it when we return. I have so many questions, but Tata says he really doesn't know all the answers right now.

When the next day arrives, Momma instructs us to wear three layers of our best clothes, because we don't know where we are going or how long we will be gone. No one knows when we will be able to do laundry. I choose my warmest clothes and Momma packs our down quilts in case it gets cold. We each pack a burlap bag with our belongings. I am excited to travel on a train for the first time, as I have never gone beyond the neighboring towns on either side of my village.

When the time comes to leave, we are all packed and ready. It is April, 1944 and Hiyasura, who is now 21, and Yutke who is 19, help Momma and Aunt Lea with the younger kids. Fischel is 16 and I am 14 years old. Petyu is 13, Blimchu is 10, Fay is 8 and

Myerbear is 6 years old. Tata and Momma lead our whole family toward the school, with each of the older kids carrying a burlap bag of belongings. There are a lot of people at the school when we arrive and all of them are Jewish.

The soldiers order us to wait in line to be processed by someone who takes down all family information. They record our birthdays and ages, address, and any valuables we want to register. When this is complete, there is nothing more to do than wait for our transport. We wait and wait for our turn to load up. No one seems happy about the train trip, so I am quiet about my feeling of excitement.

Finally, after hours of waiting, we climb into an ox-driven wagon that holds about 50 people, all standing. The ox marches very slowly to the next town, Ungvar. It takes so long that my legs get tired from standing still. There are so many people moving about the Ungvar train station that we have to be vigilant to stay together and watch the little ones.

This train station is the biggest building I've ever been in. I hear some of the adults talking about how the station transports shipments of bricks all over Europe, from the brick factory here. Momma points out that Jews from all of the neighboring villages are here in Ungvar with us. We remain in the train station for three or four weeks, under the watchful eyes of Hungarian soldiers with guard dogs. We sleep in tents at night. The soldiers remind us regularly that Jews are not to try and run away or they will be shot. Our parents continue to reassure us that we should not worry, as God will protect us.

The train station is very busy. Tata says the train cars they are using are called cattle cars which are usually used to transport animals or dry goods. Every day, more cattle cars arrive and get filled completely full with Jews. As each train leaves, I wonder where it is going and hope it is somewhere wonderful.

When our name is finally called, it's our turn to load up on the train. We are packed in like preserved pickles in a jar. Once the car is full with 60 to 80 people, they lock the doors. The car has no seats or toilets, and no water. There are small openings at the top of the car to provide air, but only those tall enough can see out and the openings do not provide enough ventilation. I am not tall enough to see out, so I have no idea where we are or where we are headed. It is colder than usual this April, and hard to stay warm, even packed together like sardines. The train does not stop for any reason, so we ride and ride for a few days, standing all the while. Momma, Aunt Lea and Tata try to comfort Petyu, Blimchu, Fay and Myerbear. Even though I feel overwhelmed, I try not to cry or complain. I want to show Momma and Tata that I am now a big girl. A group of men read their Bibles and quietly recite prayers. The cars get stinky because of the poor ventilation and no toilets. I don't understand why we are treated this way. The looks of panic on the faces of the adults and the cries of the younger children unsettle me.

At long last, the train finally slows down and comes to a stop. The door is unlocked and a man in a blue and white uniform climbs into our cattle car and tells us we are in Auschwitz, Poland. He begins telling people what to do next and helping them move their belongings. He asks me how old I am and I tell him I am 14 years old.

He murmurs, "Tell them you are 18."

Yutke is holding my little brother, Myerbear. The man asks her if this is her child. "No, he is my brother," she replies. He tells her that young children must stay with their mothers. He gives information to many people as we climb down off the cattle car.

Once on the ground, all luggage and possessions are tossed into a big pile. We are put in rows of five people and directed to walk on for about five minutes. There is no talking allowed and everyone is confused because we don't know what is coming next. When we arrive in front of three German SS Officers in uniform, they begin to separate us into groups. One of them asks me how old I am, and following the advice of the man on the train, I tell the soldier that I am 18 years old.

Hiyasura responds, "No she isn't. She is 14."

"No. I am 18," I insist.

The officers wave my sisters and me to the left. Tata and Fischel are directed to the line on the right, while Momma, Aunt Lea and my three little sisters and baby brother go forward, joining another line of people. I don't know why they are separating us, but Yutke keeps telling me to be quiet and not ask questions. "Just do what they say," she insists. The guards quickly move everyone along so that there is no time to talk to Momma or Tata. I try to keep my eyes on them as their lines move off in different directions, but I quickly lose sight of them. I wonder how long it will be until I see them again.

Maybe they separate men from women here, but that doesn't explain why Momma, Aunt Lea and the little kids went in another line. So many things are happening that don't make sense to me. My thoughts get interrupted when the soldiers yell at us to keep moving. Yutke, Hiyasura and I follow our line into a big bathroom marked Lager (Camp) C. Maybe here we will wash up after being stuck in the cattle car for days. Instead, we are ordered to take off all our clothes and toss them in a pile. I slowly remove the three dresses that Momma had me wear. I pause when I have stripped down to my underwear, and look at the many women around me. Everyone is undressing. I have never been naked in front of strangers before, and am feeling confused and humiliated. This is so wrong, but no one is saying anything. When Hiyasura and Yutke start removing their undergarments like the other women, I slowly do, too. I am shivering and feel scared. The soldiers take photographs of us, humiliating us further. I think this must be hell because I have never experienced anything worse.

I am appalled to realize that the next step is to have every hair shaved off our bodies. I cannot understand why they need to take hair off of my head, arms, legs, and even my most private places. I can see the other Jewish women don't understand what is going on either, and look ashamed. The faces of the women shaving us are like stone, showing no emotion at all. I feel so exposed with no clothes, and now, no hair to cover me. I reach up to touch my hairless head and am shocked to feel my nubby and bruised scalp from the rough handling of the emotionless woman with the razor.

After we are shaved, we are ordered to grab a drab dress from a pile on the cement floor and are given wooden clogs. The clogs seem to be all the same size and don't really fit anyone. They are hard and difficult to walk in. I have to shuffle to get anywhere. My dress hangs down to the ground, like a sack. Since my head is freezing, I tear off a piece of fabric from the bottom of my dress to wrap around my head. At least my head is covered, but I am still very cold. I don't understand why I can't retrieve my old socks and undergarments that are in a heap on the floor close by.

As soon as we are dressed, we are forced to go outside and line up for tzel appell (roll call). It is now late evening and there are so many people moving about that I get separated from my sisters. I am frightened and frantically call out their names. Two bald women in dingy dresses approach me. They reach for me and reassure me, "Roysie, its us, Yutke and Hiyasura." I hug them both fiercely and stammer, "I did not recognize you!" I am so relieved to be with them, that I can't stop shaking.

As we wait for further orders, a Polish guard with a very large and scary German Shepard stands next to Yutke. She doesn't look frightened but I know she is. We never had a dog at home and this one growls and shows his teeth unexpectedly. He could definitely hurt us. Yutke moves just a step away from the guard and his dog, confirming for me that she is scared. All of us notice a huge fire spewing heavy smoke that looks like a burning mountain across the open area from us. I can see shadows of people moving about through the smoke and can hear the cries of children. There is an overpowering, foul smell coming from the fire. Somehow, I taste the fire in my mouth.

Yutke asks the guard as she gestures towards the fire, "What is all the noise about?"

The guard responds, "They are burning hair."

Yutke replies, "Burning hair would not make such a noise."

To which he snaps, "They are burning cripples."

Yutke, Hiyasura and I are speechless. Did I just misunderstand what he said? I look at my sisters for either reassurance or answers. Yutke moves her mouth without a sound, saying, "Not one word." No one talks. The eerie silence of those surrounding us makes the screams and cries coming from the fire louder and nearly unbearable. A sick feeling comes over me as I realize the guards and soldiers are barbaric, cold-blooded animals.

We march under a sign that says, "Arbeit Macht Frei" (Work Makes Freedom). Although I don't speak German, Yiddish is a similar language and I can decipher that the sign says something about work and freedom.

Barrack 26 is our sleeping quarters. I have never seen anything like it before: dirt floors and rows of wooden three-tiered bunks. No straw-filled mattresses. No blankets or pillows. No heat. A fireplace that doesn't work. Hiyasura, Yutke and I are assigned to the top bunk with five other women. We climb up and huddle body-to-body to stay warm during the freezing cold night. I am so thankful that my sisters are with me because everything is foreign, harsh, unexplained, and unbearably cold.

The next morning, I decide to look around the camp to figure out where we are. I assure my sisters, "There are a lot of people milling around and I can blend in or hide. I will be careful."

I walk outside and I am shocked to see many barracks just like the one we slept in, arranged in rows of buildings. There are dozens of people walking around outdoors, all shaved, all shivering. Some are wandering around like zombies. When I try to talk to one of these zombie-like women, she just stares through me, doesn't answer and keeps walking. She is truly frightening to me. It is as though she is here, but not really here at all.

There is a twelve-foot electric fence encircling the camp. Dead people hang from the fence, their bodies contorted. I wonder why so many would grab onto the electric fence to end their life. What kind of hell are we in? Why are we prisoners? Feeling like a second-class citizen in Seredne was nothing compared to this.

I am on a mission to learn all I can, so I ask those who have been here longer to help me understand more. Most of the women are very patient with me asking questions because they remember how frightening and foreign everything was for them when they arrived. They explain that some people cannot endure the severity of the camp and know that if they hold on to the electrified fence, it ends their life in 20 seconds. One thing I learn for certain is no one can escape. There are guards with guns, the deadly electric fence, and people watching your every move. This must be Hell.

The half-dead zombie-like people and the bodies clinging to the electric fence are overpowering. I am in a daze seeing the true horrors of war here.

As I walk around, I think I hear my Yiddish name called out softly. How could anyone in this godforsaken place know my Yiddish name? But then I hear it again.

"Roysie!"

I turn to see a man in a striped uniform whom I do not recognize, but he is beckoning to me.

He approaches me and says, "Don't you know who I am? I'm your Tata."

With a wave of pure shock, I realize it is Tata! I am tremendously relieved. At home, Tata always wore a suit and hat, glasses, and had a beard. I look again at this man with no hair, and I know it is him. I hug him as tight as I can, cry and kiss him and kiss him some more. His arms around me are the first sense of warmth I have felt since arriving. Tata explains that he and Fischel were selected to go to work in a factory. They will leave soon, but in the meantime, he has been looking everywhere for his family. He decided we must be in this all-women's camp where the Hungarian people are sent.

"Where is your mother?" he asks.

"I don't know, but I have Yutke and Hiyasura with me."

"Whatever you do, stay together because you will have a much better chance of survival," Tata replies.

I think, "What chance does a 14 year old have of surviving in a place like this?" But I don't say anything.

Tata holds both of my arms at my side, looks me in the eyes and sternly says, "Make sure you stay alive so you can tell the world what they are doing to us."

I assure him I will do my best. Then he and I make plans for all of us to meet again tomorrow at this spot.

I run to tell Hiyasura and Yutke what just happened. They can hardly believe I met up with Tata on my attempt to find out more about the camp. They are so relieved to know he and Fischel are all right. All of us are excited to see them again tomorrow. It is hard to sleep tonight knowing our plan. The night cannot pass fast enough for me.

The next day, Yutke, Hiyasura and I wait at the designated spot to meet up with Tata and Fischel. When we see them, I cry in relief. We all hug and kiss each other, and we are so happy to have time together. Tata repeats his solemn advice to each of us.

"Do your best to stay together. Stay alive so you can tell the world what they are doing to us."

He explains that he and Fischel will leave soon for factory work, but we set up another meeting for tomorrow. We all cry and kiss again as we say goodbye. At least Tata and Fischel have each other, we agree, and so do the three of us. I hope Momma and Aunt Lea are able to remain together with the little ones. As I stand with my sisters and watch them walk away, a cold shiver runs through me. Just for a second I wonder when we will meet again, then I remind myself that it will be tomorrow at this same spot. I am sure of it.

The next day, we go to our spot to meet Tata and Fischel, as planned. We wait and wait for what seems like an eternity, but they do not come. I keep walking out and looking around one corner of a bunkhouse and another to try and catch their approach, but they must be coming from a different direction today. Hiyasura and Yutke eventually convince me they must have gone to the factory. It will be some time before we see them again, we all know. I tell my sisters that my heart feels heavy in my chest, and they agree they feel the same heaviness, but remind me to hold on to Tata's advice to stay together.

Hiyasura, Yutke, and I have no choice but to stay together in this evil place. We share a bunk bed, meals, and one bathroom with 1,000 women. No one is allowed to use the bathroom at night. It has sinks with cold running water, but no soap for us to wash up. There is no toilet, just a hole in the ground. There is nowhere to shower or take baths. We have only the one plain dress we are wearing and no way to clean it, except with the cold water. Some women in our barracks say the Germans put chemicals in our soup so none of the women will get a period. If women did menstruate, it would be a nightmare. We don't even have underwear.

Without a shower, or soap, we are constantly filthy. We are always itchy with the bites of lice and bed bugs. We can rinse out our dress and walk around naked while it dries. It doesn't really matter because we are surrounded by 28,000 women in the same predicament. We have no way to really clean our one dress and clogs. We are left to rot for four months in the same horrible dress.

I quickly realize this concentration camp has some predictable events. Every day they count us (tzel appell) as we stand in rows of five people.

At 5:00 am, guards shout, "Get up! Get up! Schnell! Schnell! (Quick! Quick!)"

We all rise and run outdoors to be counted, whether it is freezing, raining, or sunny. We stand in lines for hours three times a day until the guards have a tally, then we are released back to our barracks. I am told this is how they know how much space is available for the new people they bring in by train every day. People leave to work in factories, get killed, or are gassed, so the counting is necessary. Sometimes we are forced to kneel and hold up rocks until our arms feel like they will break and the rocks fall. Other times they make us move rocks from one spot to another, then back to the original location. It doesn't make any sense, but we don't ask questions. We keep our heads down and do what we are told because any resistance may mean we will be shot. I have seen it happen.

I continue to ask questions of others when we are in the barrack, to learn all I can about this camp. Our location is Auschwitz II-Birkenau concentration camp, in Auschwitz, Poland. I learn that there are several camps here, including one for political prisoners, called Auschwitz One. Our camp is divided into several smaller camps, called lagers, which separate categories of people with electrified fencing. We are in the transitional camp with mostly Hungarian women. There is also a Czech camp and a Gypsy camp nearby. Men are housed here temporarily. Men are collected until the desired number is reached, then they are shipped out

to forced-labor work sites. The men's barrack must be where Tata and Fischel sleep.

I cannot escape the horrible smell from the crematorium's chimney of burning bodies, 24 hours a day. The sickening stench of burning flesh makes me want to vomit, and never becomes less upsetting emotionally. The smoke and smell burn a black hole in my heart. We have to find a way out of this place, and that will require me knowing as much as possible about how it is run.

Our barrack is one of 28 barracks. There are 28,000 people in this mostly women's camp. The last two buildings, numbers 29 and 30, are the bathroom and the kitchen. The people working in the camp are all Jews. That is why the man who helped us get off the train gave me such good advice. He is a Jewish prisoner himself, being forced to work in the camp. Only the guards here are not Jewish.

The women explain that prisoners are chosen for jobs and they must comply. Any Jewish worker who resists is shot dead on the spot. Strong Jewish women (called Kapos) are put in charge of running each barrack. The Kapos live amongst us in the barrack and watch everything. They are not paid, but they have certain rights that others lack. They may get more food, but they are doing the dirty work for the Germans. The cooks preparing the meals are Jewish, as well. Jews clean out the bathroom barrack that is used by 28,000 women. Jews even work the gas chamber. These poor souls send their own people to their death every day. If their family members arrive in line, they have to send them to their death. This is too much for me to process, and I begin to see why some people touch the electric fence to end their misery.

I ask repeatedly why we can hear people crying out near the crematorium. I learn that when a group is gassed in the "showers," not all the people are dead when they burn the bodies. Maybe they don't give them enough gas, because we can hear the screaming coming from the crematorium. The men running the incinerators, called sonderkommandos, will be sent into them soon, so they cannot tell the world what is happening.

One day, I ask a woman why I haven't seen my mother, aunt, my little sisters, and brother. The lady is careful to gently tell me what I already think I know. She sadly affirms that my worst fears are correct. When they got off the train they were put in a line that led directly to the gas chamber. As Hiyasura, Yutke and I weep for our family, she explains the Germans see elderly, disabled, pregnant women, mothers and children as a liability. They cannot work and produce for the Third Reich (The German State), so they are exterminated. This is why the sorting happens when the trains arrive at Auschwitz II-Birkenau. They also remind me of how lucky I was to be accepted as being 18 and eligible for the adult factory work line. If the sorters had known I was 14, I would have gone with my mother and aunt and younger siblings straight to the gas chamber.

I do not feel lucky in any way right now. I just can't get used to the idea that my mother, three sisters, and little brother are gone. It is beyond comprehension. When Yutke, Hiyasura and I try to talk about it, we cannot speak. We just cry. We have to keep going, like Tata told us to. It will eventually get better, we believe. We need to have hope.

I have difficulty processing all of this and have to keep asking myself Why? Why? Why? One of the ladies hugs me close and says, "You will never understand what these Germans are doing because it is beyond comprehension. It does not make sense and it never will. They are crazy, out of their minds. You are not. Remember, you are the sane one here. Go where you need to inside of yourself and remember who you are. They cannot steal your soul unless you give it to them. Never give them your soul. Follow their rules and survive so that the real you can blossom again when you are free. War is a horrible thing, but it will end. When it does, there is another life for you outside of Auschwitz II-Birkenau and you need to live for that."

I know she is right so I listen, leaning into her for support. My mother would have told me similar things. Right now, all I can do is cry because she cannot tell me herself. My family is forever changed and I wonder for a moment, what else can happen. Then I remind myself everyone here has to live with their losses. In this, I am not alone.

I wake every morning into what seems like another nightmare.

The only thing we get for breakfast is black coffee. We have no plates, cups or utensils. When the kitchen staff bring pots of coffee to the barracks, we pass the pot around our group of 10 to 12 women. The coffee is so horrible that I can barely drink it. It tastes like the black soot that is left after a fire burns out. It makes me nauseous. Many of us cannot drink the coffee, even though we are genuinely hungry and thirsty. We are literally starving.

Lunch is nothing but of a piece of bread. Occasionally, they will give us butter to put on it. The bread is dry and hard and we are told they put sawdust in it. We line up outdoors to get our bread at a table staffed by the kitchen women. We do not share our bread. It is coveted and sometimes hidden away for later. The food tastes horrible and is not enough to live on. It is not surprising that some prisoners here have a German nickname, "Muselmann" which means skeletal or skin and bones. So many people are too thin and I am becoming one of them.

At dinner time, we get a pot of soup to share among a dozen women. It is watery and has only a few scraps of vegetables in it. I am lucky to get a piece of cabbage or a potato in my swallow when the pot makes it to me. The majority of the sparse vegetables are near the bottom, but the problem with the bottom of the pot is the amount of sand that is always there. One thing I am sure to get in my soup is sand.

We are hungry every day. There is never enough to eat. I keep trying to find out more about the camp to see what our options might be. One night, I sneak behind the kitchen and dig through the trash cans for food. I find some potato peels and a bone to suck on. It becomes a regular habit of mine to forage for scraps behind the kitchen. I take back any scraps I find to share with my sisters. We agree to tell no one. If others find the scraps, there will be none for us.

I have not made many friends here, because the people keep changing. We have selections three to four times a week, where the German SS officers choose who will move on to a factory for work.

An officer comes into the barrack and shouts, "I need 300 women for selection for factory work."

Many women hurry outside to be selected. Anything must be better than this place. Once they line up, everyone removes their clothes so the officers can examine their physique, to decide if they are healthy and strong enough to do factory work. If a woman is too weak or thin, they label her as Muselmann and send her to the gas chamber.

I don't know if it is because of the food or illness, but I have a bad bout of diarrhea and am very weak. I can't stand or walk for the first few weeks of my illness. Yutke and Hiyasura will not go out to be selected without me, so we hide when the officers call for volunteers. It's not hard to hide with 1,000 people in the barrack and they only need 200 or 300 women. The officers do not notice me. This works for three or four weeks, but I am just skin and bones now. I know I need to be selected for a factory to get out of here.

Yutke and Hiyasura help me stand and pinch my cheeks so I look like I have some color. The problem comes when I undress. I am so frightened because I know I am too thin and weak to be chosen. My worst fear comes true when the officers call me "Muselmann" and send me to the gas chamber line.

It is a torturous few minutes walking to that line. My sisters help me get there, holding me under the arms as we cry in panic. There is so much going on around us that I begin to wonder if we can somehow sneak away. I tell Yutke and Hiyasura what I am thinking and we agree to try it. We have no other choice.

At the agreed-upon moment, we calmly step out of the line and head straight back to our barrack. All of our hearts are pumping wildly. If an SS officer notices, we will be shot on the spot. Luckily, there are a lot of women moving about the camp and no one notices. The relief of knowing we made it back safely to the barrack is overwhelming. All of us huddle quietly on our bunk in fear that someone is coming any minute to say they caught us. As the time slowly ticks by, our fears begin to lessen. We are very lucky today, but we realize this cannot keep happening because we will surely get caught.

Food is such a problem for all of us, but particularly for me since I am too thin. At lunch one day, we stand in line outside to get our bread, as usual. The Kapo gives me my piece of bread, which I notice is half the usual size. I am so hungry that I speak without thinking,

"My bread is cut in half," I accuse her.

The Kapo is furious with me because my accusation can get her in a lot of trouble with the Germans. She pulls me out of line and takes me to where the German SS officers will be sure to see her actions. She beats me so brutally that I cannot stand for three days afterwards. My sisters are both concerned and frustrated with me for getting into trouble.

Yutke tells me, "Next time just shut up. Don't ever complain about anything again. It will only get you in trouble. Do you want to get shot?"

I know she is right, but I struggle at the injustice. We are already starving. How can they steal half of my meager food? Still, I need to learn to keep my mouth shut.

Today, good fortune is upon us. One of the ladies in Barrack 26 tells us that we have cousins in Barrack 3. We are shocked and all three of us begin asking questions in rapid succession. What are their names? How did you find them? Are you sure? How did you figure out we are related?

When we give them time to respond fully, we realize it is true that our Bohm cousins on Momma's side, Dora and her daughter Handa Josipovitz, are indeed here! Even better news for us is that they help dispense food. This is a wonderful coincidence. Surely, they will help me get extra food to gain some of my weight back.

Yutke and Hiyasura help me sneak over to Barrack 3 on the premise that we are going to the bathroom. To our surprise, the guards do not even notice when we change barracks. Here in Barrack 3, my cousins are in charge of the whole barrack, including food distribution. They help me get extra food every day and I begin to gain weight and think more clearly. It literally saves my life to have a little more food. I am so thankful to be with them in this horrible place.

I even find a pair of pants left by a prisoner who died. I put them on for warmth, but have trouble sleeping with them on. My

sisters tell me to lie still and stop moving around so much.

I try to stop fidgeting, but I just cannot. I am so itchy. The next morning, my sisters discover that the pants are full of lice that bit me all night, so as much as I like the warmth, the pants must go. Thankfully, we are entering the summer months so it is not quite as cold.

As the months go slowly by, in September of 1944, we notice that Auschwitz II-Birkenau begins to empty out. Our cousins are taken to work in a factory and we are so sad to see them go. As the barracks' residents dwindle, it makes our exit more urgent. Now that there are less people to hide among, we are at risk of being noticed. I am getting stronger and less skeletal, so I urge my sisters to try selection with me, but yet again, I am labeled as Muselmann and sent to the gas chamber line.

At least I can get out of the line on my own now, and head back to the barrack. I do this repeatedly enough that we decide that I can no longer go through the selection process at all. Sooner or later I will be caught sneaking away from the line and be shot. There has to be another way out.

"We have to get out of here," repeats over and over in my mind. I know we cannot give up, because I have hope. I always remember what my father told me. Stay together because your chances of survival will be much better.

It is not easy to keep hope alive while we are in camp. Giving up seems easier, and we see many who do give up, and end up on the electric fencing. There are a few good rumors that help us have hope. Women gather in the bathroom to hear the latest rumor that the Americans or Russians may liberate us. The hope that we will reunite with Tata and Fischel keeps us alive. Even with this hope, it is hard to continue believing in something. We all question our faith in God. How could God allow this to happen? Following all the Jewish laws got us nowhere.

One day in October 1944, the SS officers arrive at the barracks announcing they need 300 women to go to a German factory in Freudenthal. This is the day that Yutke, Hiyasura and I will be chosen. I know it.

As we are preparing to line up, I look at my sisters and tell them, "Go get selected and save me a place in line. I will find a way to sneak into the group."

Hiyasura and Yutke both look worried, but go out the front door and get selected. I must find a way to get in line without being detected. Meanwhile I am working feverishly to come up with a plan to join them. Our barracks are always guarded by the Kapos, no matter what. My heart races so loudly I wonder if others can hear it, as I try to figure out what to do. I don't have much time; I must think fast.

I watch a woman, who gives out food from the kitchen, as she exits the back of the barrack. Suddenly, I find myself running as fast as I can down the long hallway of the barrack toward the back door. The female Kapo guarding the door raises her hand to stop me. My heart is beating hard in my chest as she looks at me.

"You can't go out this door. You have to go out that way to be selected for work," she says, pointing in the opposite direction.

"I don't want to go to work," I say shaking my head. "My mother has just gone out that door and I need to go with her," as I point to the door behind her.

The seconds that pass before she responds feel like hours. I continue to reach toward the door, imploring her to help me. Somehow, the Kapo takes pity on me and lets me out the door. I scan the area for guards as I sneak around the building to join my sisters in line. There are enough people moving about that no one sees me enter the group. I can see my sisters and they have a spot for me to slide into. I feel a sense of freedom for the first time in a long time. Suddenly, I know I am strong and brave. It is as though an angel is looking after me, I think, as I look upward. Maybe it's my mother who helps me out of this terrible situation. Maybe things will get better for us now.

I make eye contact with Hiyasura. She has sheer joy on her face as I approach. She elbows Yutke to indicate that I am on my way over. As I enter the line, Yutke immediately grabs my arm and squeezes it so tight. All of us are frightened and excited at the same time. Hiyasura and Yutke are relieved that I am with them, and even a little surprised that I made it. I can see the questions on their faces, but silently indicate that we can't talk about it now. I will explain how I did this later, when we are alone. The three of us try to act calm so no one will notice that I am not supposed to be in line. I squeeze their hands as tight as I can, so tight that I can't feel my own fingers. We have to celebrate internally and happiness springs up inside me. Hope and fear are at war within me.

Before leaving the camp for the factory, we need to go through a cleaning process. We know we all smell. I remember when I first came to the camp, I smelled a sour and pungent odor everywhere, on everyone. I guess I've smelled it for so long now that I don't notice it anymore, but you can always see the revulsion on the faces of new prisoners when they arrive. It is the stench of death on living bodies. I can see the dirt in the lines on people's faces, our hands don't come clean when we rinse them. The hair that grew back in the last four months is stuck to our heads and has a foul odor. It is clear to me that we are not supposed to have been here this long. But now that time will end, if I can make it through cleaning without being labeled a Muselmann.

The guards march us to the cleaning place where we prepare to leave for the work camp. I am shaking with fear that if I take my clothes off I will be sent to the gas chamber. I clasp my hands together to try and calm my shaking, but it doesn't work. No matter how hard I try, my fear shows. I know that this may give me away, so my mind whirls as I try to think of something. I whisper to Yutke and Hiyasura that this is my greatest fear. I am still too skinny and if they make me take off my clothes, they will see that I am not strong enough to work. I try again to control my shaking and act brave for my sisters' sakes. We have to stay together, like Tata told us.

Yutke and Hiyasura reassure me, "We are leaving together, and soon. Stay calm and do what they say."

We enter the bathroom, which is just as dirty as we are. My teeth start to chatter and I clench my jaw to ensure that no one knows how afraid I am.

"Remove your clothes," a Kapo yells. I hesitantly take my dress off with shaking hands.

It has been so long since I have had a shower that I'm almost afraid of it. This doesn't last long when I realize we finally have soap to wash our bodies! I had no idea how wonderful it could feel to wash from head to toe with soap. The lather quickly turns brown so I rinse it off and lather up again. I hear soft sighing coming from many of the women who are having the same amazing experience in the shower.

Next, they shave our entire bodies again. I haven't grown much hair since they shaved my head originally, but I had become fond of what I did have. It made me feel more human, but I am so numb by the time they get to me, that I stand still without complaint as they shave me again.

Fortunately, no one says anything about my skeletal appearance. I try to blend into the crowd so no one will notice me, but when I am shaved, it is obvious. Yet, the woman who shaves me says nothing. As I walk out, I breathe a sigh of relief that no one has apparently noticed my skinny body. The Jewish women working in this area must have taken pity on me as I clung to my sisters. Once we are showered and shaven, the next step is to get disinfected to kill the lice.

The Kapo has a metal dispenser that creates a powder when she depresses the handle. It sprays disinfectant out in a wide arc, landing on my skin and leaving a white dusting. We stand still and say nothing as she makes sure to cover every area of our bodies. The white powder burns like fire on my cold, freshly shaved skin. I want to rub it off my body, but the Kapos yell that we must leave it on us for it to work. No one resists or removes the powder. The thought of being free of lice and bed bugs helps me stay still.

Finally, we are given decent street clothes to wear. It is the first time in four months that I have changed my clothes. One of the women pins a piece of paper with a number on it to my dress. She tells me that this will be the number that identifies me from now on. They have taken away my name. I am no longer Roysie, or even a Schwartz. Now I am just a number: A25893.

Although they have taken away my name, they treat me more like a human. They need me for my labor, so I am instantly more valuable than when I was just a bag of bones waiting for death at

Auschwitz II-Birkenau. I feel hopeful that our next location will be better, although nothing could be worse than Auschwitz II-Birkenau.

We move outside and are told to form a line. I stay close to my sisters. At the end of the line, there is a table of Jewish women processing those moving to the factory.

"Give your name, address, and the number on your shirt," someone yells at me.

Once we are processed by the women, we are loaded into a big truck which drives out of the camp. As we pass through the gates, I feel an incredible weight lift off my shoulders. This is truly a moment to remember. I know that my life may not be any easier at the work factory, but at least we are alive. We are scared and weak, but we have left the Hell of Auschwitz II-Birkenau behind us.

On the ride in the truck, I whisper to Hiyasura and Yutke how I managed to get out of the barrack and sneak into the factory line with them. We are so relieved to be together, in a truck, leaving the camp. It doesn't take long to get to the factory. We quickly learn that our destination, Bruntal, Czechoslovakia, or Freudenthal as the Germans call it, is a sub-camp of Auschwitz II-Birkenau. It contains sleeping quarters for the women on the grounds of a masonry textile mill. The Emerich Machold textile mill produces fabric, German uniforms, ammunition and gas masks.

At the factory, they provide us with more decent street clothes similar to what I previously owned. They are clean and presentable. We also get shoes and stockings, a canteen to share, a cup, fork and a spoon. We are fed three small meals that never fill us up, and though they are not great, they are better than the sandy soup and stale bread we had before.

Our lodging is a stone block, two-story building just a five-minute walk to and from the factory. We sleep in a large open room with the beds lined up against the walls. The building is cold, so we go to bed fully dressed. Even our blankets are not enough to keep us warm, but at least we have blankets. One of the women explains that she overheard a guard talking about how their goal was only to keep the pipes from freezing. Any additional heat produced would be a waste of resources. Our comfort is not of their concern. The building has a musty odor, but I have my own bed with a mattress, sheets, blankets and a pillow. We are allowed access to the bathrooms at night. We even get a shower with soap and are given clean clothes once a week. The showers and bathroom are just down the hall. Compared to the Hell of Auschwitz II-Birkenau, this feels like Heaven.

Each day we have roll call before leaving for the factory. We still need to line up and be accounted for, but this counting is far different from Auschwitz II-Birkenau. We are just being counted to be sure all are present. There is no harm or additional discomfort inflicted upon us with hours of standing or kneeling for no reason. They are not beating us. The Jewish Kapos continue to live amongst us and keep us in line, especially in front of the German soldiers. Even the Kapos are not brutal, as before, and allow us some freedoms.

Although our living situation is much better than Auschwitz II-Birkenau, we do not forget that we are still slaves to the Germans. We work 10 to 12 hours a day, six days per week, without any pay, and our lodging is surrounded by an eight-foot tall fence. The fence is not electrified like the one at Auschwitz II-Birkenau, but no one is strong enough to climb it. I can hear the wind whistle through the chain link and feel the stares of the German guards as they walk us to and from our work each day. The guards do not scream at us like they did at Auschwitz II-Birkenau, but we are definitely still prisoners.

On our first day of work at Freudenthal, the numbers that were pinned to our clothes are tattooed onto our left forearms. I know that I should feel the pain, but I don't, as I watch them scratch the needle across my skin. In my mind, I am thinking about the law that Jews may not make any cuttings or print any marks on their bodies. How will God take this new development? I am not in any position to resist the permanent tattoo that reminds me every single day that I am not free. A25893 is emblazoned for the world to see every time I reach my hand out to touch my sister or grab a piece of machinery. Each day as we leave the factory, we show our tattoo which confirms that we are Jews who belong in the camp, and not one of the free citizens who goes home every night.

At the factory, we work with local German women who were free civilians living in Czechoslovakia before the war (German expatriates) and a few old German men, who did not go to war. They are our supervisors and schedule our work. They treat us fairly but are not overly kind to us. We only discuss work assignments with them. Everyone has an assignment and as long as they do it well, the supervisors leave us alone. Everyone works the same hours and gets the same meals.

Sometimes the German lady who works next to me brings me an apple. It is a big risk for her to offer me any special treatment, because she could be labeled a Jewish sympathizer and be taken to jail or shot. It is also a risk for me because I can be labeled a thief. There are no apples given to Jews here, so how would I get one? It would be up to a guard to decide my fate if I were caught with an apple. We are very careful that no one of authority is around when she hands me the apple. I think she realizes how hard our lives are and feels a bit sorry for me. It is so good to see the humanity in some people, because we have lived for months, and some of us for years, surrounded by inhumane and savage guards every day. We have been treated as though we are not human.

While some workers are kind, there continues to be an ongoing threat from the German Nazi officers. They yell at us, and remind us that if we don't do quality work, we will go back to "the killing place." My very existence has been threatened so many times, that it is less intense now when they threaten us, even though I know that if I disobey, I die.

My sisters and I are separated during the day because each of us has a different job within the factory. Every morning Yutke and Hiyasura remind me to stay quiet, keep my head down, and do my work to avoid trouble. I reassure them that I am wiser now and will not speak out. As we enter the factory, Yutke moves to the area with ammunition. Her job is to assemble the bullets once they are filled with gunpowder. Hiyasura spends her day sewing. She says it's fine, but she would rather sew almost anything other than German uniforms.

I inspect gas masks. I am not sure why they assigned this job to me. I don't know anything about gas masks. I know that they are supposed to protect you from chemical attacks, but before I went to Auschwitz II-Birkenau, I never imagined needing one. Now, I sometimes think about all the Jews that might have lived if they wore a gas mask as they walked into the gas chamber. It is hard for me to think that Germans might use these masks to protect themselves while killing Jews. I just keep telling myself that I am only one person. I cannot stop the Germans alone and if I resist, I will be killed. I cannot understand why the rest of the world is not coming to stop Hitler. It seems they are facilitating his program by being silent.

I feel lucky that I am short, because I get to sit on a tall stool to be level with the stack of masks. Everyone else must stand. I work all day inspecting gas masks to make sure they are made well. I can't help thinking it might be good if the mask is inferior for a German soldier to use. It makes me smile on the inside to think the soldier might not survive because I made them a faulty gas mask. I am wiser now and can contain my feelings, appearing to be diligently working. Just keep things moving and avoid trouble with the guards, I tell myself. I am always afraid that if I attract the attention of the guards, they will realize that I am too skinny to work and will kill me. Then who will help my sisters stay together? I have to stay alive and do as Tata said.

After a month at the factory, I gather the courage to speak to the person in charge. I take a deep breath before approaching the intimidating officer. My hands shake as he looks down at me. I am still very short for my 14 years and with no heels or hair to help me seem taller, I am sure that I look like a younger child.

"This is hard work," I say, shocked at how confident my voice sounds. Because my hands are shaking I press them into my sides, hoping he won't notice. "I should get an extra meal to conserve my strength."

To my utter surprise, the officer allows me an extra meal each day. On the first day, I gobble it up, still amazed that I am given this precious gift of extra rations. The next day, I hide it to take to the living quarters so I can share it with my sisters. We are all so thankful for the extra rations because the meals never fill us up. Though I am the youngest, Tata tasked me with keeping us together and staying alive to tell the world. I feel it is my job to make sure that we all survive.

Each night after work, we walk back to our living quarters escorted by the German SS guards who wear machine guns. When we return from the factory, we wash up with basins of water at the end of the long rows of beds. We cannot socialize with the other prisoners at work, but they allow us to socialize together after dinner. Most days we are so tired from working long hours in the factory, that we only have a brief time to talk and relax. In the evenings, we build friendships, dream of life after the war and hope for something better. I make friends with Rivka, another Hungarian Jew who is my age. She is like me, always looking for news about our release or some scrap of information that could help us later.

Over time, my sisters and I realize the German doctors in white coats conduct experiments on prisoners. I don't remember the incident, but my sisters tell me I was taken by one of the doctors for several hours. Upon my return, my mouth remained painful for several days. I ask my sisters to look in my mouth to find out why it was so sore. They notice that all my teeth are drilled out and filled with something gray that looks like street cement. I cannot see inside my mouth because we have no mirrors, but I had no fillings in my teeth before coming to Freudenthal. The procedure is so awful, I block it out. It takes weeks for the pain to subside.

We get bits of news from the German ladies we work with at the factory when the guards are out of sight. Hearing that the Russians and Americans are coming to liberate us soon helps us to hold on. I learn from them that there are almost 300 of us Jewish women working as slaves in the German factory. Since hardly anyone leaves Freudenthal, the women I live and work with become like family as we spend weeks and months together.

At the factory, the guards thankfully do not shave our hair as it is now late winter and the weather has turned very cold. One day, I wake up and realize that my hair has grown out so much that it falls into my eyes. I pull it down below my eyes, marveling that it is long enough for me to see it. The dark locks that now barely cover the top of my forehead remind me of a young boy in our village. I am thankful for anything to cover the bare skin of my scalp. I remember with longing the days when my mother would gently help me wash my hair and brush it for me. It's one of the few fond memories of my mother I still carry with me.

Our daily lives continue as each and every day we wake, eat, work, walk back to our quarters, wash, eat, and sleep. It seems a never-ending monotony, but we are grateful for it. This routine feels safe. Auschwitz II-Birkenau had no predictability since any situation could turn into a nightmare in a second. Safety is rare these days, so we embrace it as much as possible. The guards mostly leave us alone unless someone steps out of line. Hardly any of us do that anymore because we all recognize that there is safety in submission.

Our old living quarters are musty and need repairs regularly with 300 women using them daily. This is a problem because we don't know how to repair things ourselves. At home, Tata or Fischel fixed everything, but we had none of these modern devices in Seredne. One day, I am in the bathroom when I hear SS Officers discussing how they will get repairs completed in the residence. They want to get them done without having to do it themselves, by using American Prisoners of War (POWs).

One German officer says, "These POWs may be protected by the Geneva Convention, but we can use them for simple repairs here. They need to earn their keep by working. If they can't, then maybe we will treat them the same as Jews who can't work."

The officers laugh and move on so I cannot hear their conversation any longer.

The POWs are kept near us in Freudenthal, but not where we can see them, since our work camps are divided by an eight-foot tall fence. When we have a broken faucet, toilet, shower, bed, or anything else, the Germans send a POW to repair it. We never know when they are scheduled to come.

The first time a POW comes to our building for repairs, he is accompanied by a German guard or Kapo. The POW is a handsome young man with pretty brown hair and brown eyes. He is thin, but not nearly as thin as we are. He has a spring in his step that none of us have. He is clearly not a German as he is treated like a prisoner. The guard barks orders at him and he quietly complies. Mostly he keeps his head down and does his work, but I notice he steals a glance at us when the guard is distracted. He lifts his chin to acknowledge us and I think I see a flash of a smile on his face. I must have imagined that. No stranger has smiled at me in at least a year. This man is taking quite a chance by trying to communicate with us. The guard will certainly punish him if he knows. All of us act as though he is not there. As soon as they are gone, I ask my sisters if they noticed him looking at us. They did not.

"He could be shot for interacting with us! He would not do that," they insist. I agree, they are probably right. I must have imagined it.

The next time we need repairs, they send the same POW. When he arrives, I remind my sisters to watch closely without being noticed. We do not know who he is, but he is wearing a uniform that has spots of greens and browns all over it. It looks like the forest. We decide this design is to help camouflage him. The guard is watchful initially, but then lights a cigarette and relaxes across the room. This is when the worker makes eye contact with me again and clearly smiles, though briefly. My sisters see it and try to act calm, but they are surprised. He goes on about his work without a word or any other contact, and the guard escorts him out when he is done.

There is growing excitement among those who noticed his communication with me. Did he really smile at me? Is he to be trusted? Did we imagine it? Many of us decide that he can be trusted because he is a prisoner as well and has put himself in great danger by trying to communicate with us. Those who did not witness it are quite skeptical but agree to watch closely the next time he visits.

When the same POW returns again, the guard is even more relaxed and wanders off for a bit. One of the older women offers to stand at the doorway to keep watch for the guard. When she gives the signal that all is clear, we initiate trying to communicate. Immediately, it is apparent that we don't speak the same language. He has an interesting accent, but we cannot decipher his words. We quickly learn to communicate with gestures and a lot of guessing.

He points to himself and says, "Joe," then points to one of us. No one answers initially, so I step forward and say, "Roysie" as I point to myself. He gives a wonderful smile in response. Joe holds up his little container of tools to show us he is here to work as he makes his way to our broken toilet. We are excited to have a worker who seems kind and friendly.

While he is working, all of us chatter excitedly though quietly. For many of us, this is the first person since we were taken from our homes who has tried to be friendly and shown kindness. Some of us agree to try cautiously to communicate with him. Some are too shy or still suspicious of him, however, others are willing to tell Joe their names as well. When he comes out of the bathroom, Rivka points to herself and steps forward, telling him her name. He smiles, says her name and bends down low mimicking a curtsy, to acknowledge her. With each person that gives him her name, he smiles broadly, repeats the name, and bows down, making us giggle. We must be careful that no guards witness these moments of communication because we will all be subject to punishment. It is hard to worry about that now when we are actually having fun.

Each time we need a repair, we hope the guards will send Joe. Joe has proven his ability with repairs, because they always send him. Sometimes we even break something just to have Joe come. One day, Joe motions me toward the trashcan as he leaves our room. No one understands why, but we begin searching the area and I find a chocolate bar that Joe left in the trashcan. I am thrilled. I have a decision to make. What do I do with the chocolate? Should I eat it, hide it or share it? I decide to share the candy with my sisters later when we are alone.

There is a note with the chocolate bar. It is printed in another language which we don't speak, but all of us begin trying to solve our little mystery message from Joe. Although most of us cannot decipher it, we smile at the thought that he wants to talk to us.

The next time Joe is assigned for repairs, he brings me another chocolate bar. I cannot understand how he has chocolate, so I gesture my question to him. He tries to answer using gestures. With his arm high up, he indicates a plane flying far and landing.

Then he pretends he is carrying a box which he opens and pulls out food and eats it while rubbing his stomach and moaning pleasantly. All the while, we are talking amongst ourselves trying to interpret his pantomime. We think he received a package from home with these chocolate bars inside it.

We all share the chocolate bar this time, which is sweet beyond words. Joe smiles as we moan just like he did in the pantomime. I forgot how good candy tastes. I remember Tata bringing home candy in his pocket after work. Yutke, Hiyasura and I share a knowing look. I know they are thinking the same thing. The sweet chocolate and fond memory makes us momentarily happy. Joe has helped us see that not everyone is evil, not everyone thinks we are less-than-human.

We talk endlessly amongst ourselves about the idea of getting a package from home. Each of us dreams of what we would like. Hiyasura talks about books and the smell of printed paper. Yutke talks about beautiful fabrics and how they feel on your hands and body. I would want a hot loaf of Momma's fresh bread with butter that someone else churned. Our happy thoughts and day dreams are a big part of how we retain our hope for the future. Without them, we might be lost.

In reality, we all know we cannot get anything by mail. Even if we could, there is no one to send things to us. My whole family was taken. My aunts, uncles, cousins and grandparents all were taken to the ghetto or Auschwitz. If a package was somehow sent to us, surely the Germans would steal it. It is very kind of Joe to share his special treats with us. We decide that it must be something to do with this Geneva Convention the guards talked about, that makes it possible for the POWs to receive packages from home.

Without real dreams of a package arriving from home, our talks about the Russians or Americans coming to liberate us is our main hope for the future. The German women we work with sneak details to us when guards are away, during work. We live for these updates and pray for the sound of airplanes overhead or bombing that will indicate they are coming. The news is intermittent and sounding better for our eventual release and liberation.

After eight months of working and living at the factory,

something starts to change. I start to feel eyes watching me steadily. I've always known that the guards watch us, but never felt this kind of observation. I can feel their eyes on me, watching like a hawk, waiting for me to make a mistake. I think they are planning to take me back to the camp and to my death. One day, I am looking through the glass of a gas mask when Rivka appears in front of me distorted by the glass. I am so startled that I jump off my stool.

"What are you doing? They will see you," I hiss at her. She should not leave her place on the line. Surely a guard will discover her and we will both get in trouble.

"Have you heard?" she asks in a whisper.

"Heard what?" I ask, confused. No one spoke to me at all today, apart from my supervisor who barks orders at us once every hour.

"We are to be marched," she says gravely. I have no idea what she means by that, but from her face I know it is not good.

"Marched where?" I ask. "By whom?"

"I don't know. I heard some guards talking about how the Russians are coming," she replies.

The word "Russians" makes my heart beat faster. I know that they are fighting against the Germans for liberation. But what does liberation look like? No one knows. All we know is that right now, the Russians are the only people who want to get us out of this prison.

A few days pass and nothing happens. I try to forget about what Rivka said, but rumors of a march are multiplying. I realize that it might be true. Fear runs cold through my veins. Who will be chosen to go? Will I be separated from my sisters?

On May 6, 1945, we wake-up to a gray, gloomy morning and prepare for work. There is an odd energy running through the room as we make our way to the door to line up. I wonder why everyone is so jittery. Are there extra guards outside? Are they moving us? Are we going on the march?

We line up in front of the door like always, but instead of the silence that usually permeates the air, whispers fly along the line.

"What is happening?" someone asks.

"Are they sending us back to the camps?"

"I don't know. Where are the guards?" "They should be here by now," another person answers.

One brave soul ventures to the door after about fifteen minutes. All of us are nervous. She opens the door and we see no one. The usually locked door swings open without resistance. We cautiously move out into the yard and find the gates to our quarters wide open. This has never happened before and all of us are very worried. We look around for guards as we walk toward the gate. There, on the fence, is a plain white bed sheet.

Someone wrote on it in German. It reads:

"There will be no work for a few days. There will be a march that all of you will be in. Wait here until we come for you."

For a moment, we all stand in shock. What does this mean? Why leave the gate open if they want us to stay here? Why didn't a guard come and tell us this information?

So many thoughts are swirling in my head. I have no idea what this means. I worry that we will be forced to march to a place that is scarier than this. If ever there is a safe place in this Hell, I believe that this factory is it. I don't want to leave, but if it means staying with my sisters, I will.

Though we all wonder what is going on, we obey the sign. Three hundred women spend two full days wondering where we will march to, why will we move and what our new jobs will be. Many wonder if we will get separated from our new friends and family. The next morning, on May 8, 1945 there is a palpable tension amongst our group as we try to balance fear with hope for a solution. Out of nowhere there is a series of rapid short pops nearby.

"Guns! Everyone get down!" someone yells.

Everyone ducks their heads or hides under a bed. I lay down on the floor next to my sisters. My own hands are shaking as I grip their hands to make sure that we stay together. I hear a loud noise outside that I have never heard before.

"Airplanes," someone says from far off to my right.

I hear people shouting in a foreign language. Suddenly I think back to what Rivka said a few days ago. Maybe it is the Russians!

Just as suddenly as it begins, the noise stops. It's as if the entire world goes quiet, waiting for the next shoe to drop. For one perfect moment, everyone is suspended in the silence. In the next moment, everything happens all at once. Women whisper and my blood pumps in my veins. I realize that I can't stay here. I am through waiting for the next bad thing to happen.

"Someone should do something!" A woman whispers just loud enough for us all to hear. When no one does anything, I know that I am the one to go. We need to know what is out there. If it is death, so be it, but if it is the Russians, it may be life.

"I will go," I say quietly to my sisters and those around us.

"Roysie, no," my sisters plead. Their voices are quiet, but the whites of their eyes glow brightly in the gloom of our barracks. I can tell by the way they grip my hands tighter that they are frightened I will die. My hands shake as I hold theirs, but I need to know what is going on.

"I will go. I will see what is out there and come back."

As I speak, I can hear Tata's voice in my head saying "Stay together no matter what." But I know that this time I must go, so that we can live.

Letting go of my sisters' hands, I make my way cautiously to the door. I cannot feel my fingers as they turn the door knob. The door creaks as I open it just enough to peer outside. Surprisingly, everything looks the same. There are no giant holes in the ground from the bombs and no people slain. The birds are still stinging in the trees, just as they do every morning. Our whole world was threatened, yet nothing has changed.

I open the door more fully, and take one step outside, into the sunlight. As I walk into the yard, the first thing I notice is the wide open gate.

"Maybe they will march us out today," I think as I walk slowly toward the gate. Beyond it, in the field, I see people moving. I crouch lower to the ground and continue to move forward in case they are Germans.

I keep waiting for a soldier to spot me and call out, but none do. I look around me at our living quarters and realize that there are no German soldiers around at all. This is the first time we are unsupervised since we left home. I feel an odd sensation begin to take root in my chest. I haven't felt it in a while and refuse to name it in case it is not real. It is the feeling of hope.

I quickly squash it down and tell myself the Germans are just outside the gate. They are waiting for me to step out of line so they can punish me. I slowly step to the opening of the gate and look out. I see men in brown uniforms walk among the corn and wheat stalks. I listen to them yell out to each other as they walk toward me. They speak a language that sounds similar to the languages we spoke at home, Czech, Hungarian and Yiddish. These must be the Russians. They are here to save us!

I want to talk to the Russians, but I know they might think I am the enemy in my German street clothes. Russians shoot Germans, so I try to think of a way to approach them safely. While scouring for ideas, I notice a stick on the ground. I grab it and tear off a piece of my dress to tie to the stick. Now my heart is beating so hard, it feels like it will split open. It is time to be decisive, I tell myself, despite my fear. So, I raise the stick and wave my torn flag of surrender at the Russians.

When they see my flag, the Russians move toward me with smiles. Smiles! My heart can hardly take this intense feeling, as it beats so fast. This could be a trick, but I don't think so. The feeling of hope in my chest spreads quickly and propels me to act. I hope the soldiers can understand my simple words:

"We are prisoners, Jews. Please help us."

The men welcome me, smile, pick me up and hug me. I am overjoyed at their response. They understand my words and are here to rescue us, I am sure. My heart is beating so hard and the feeling of relief and hope fills my chest completely. I am safe at last. It is time to tell everyone.

Immediately I guide them toward our living quarters.

"We are 300 women here." I lead them inside of the quarters and begin calling, "Girls, girls come quick! It is good news! Everyone gather together, its okay."

Women hurry toward me with questioning looks. Some stay back in fear. Soldiers are not a good thing usually, but this time is different. The soldiers take a moment to realize there are so many of us, then announce to all the women, "The war is over. You are free!"

I notice one soldier is near tears and understand these men truly care about us. He is staring at our thin arms and legs. Maybe he sees that we have been treated horribly. I realize these are good people.

This is the moment we have dreamed of, hoped for and waited long months to see. It is as wonderful as any of the dreams I had. All of us are overjoyed at the news we have waited so long to hear. Hiyasura, Yutke, and I are survivors! We stayed together like Tata said because it would improve our chance of surviving. He was right.

We hold hands and jump up and down. Everyone is crying, dancing, and laughing. The soldiers just stand and watch. They are very kind to us and bring in necessities for everyone. They offer us many types of food and clothes.

They find chickens at some of the local empty homes and kill them for us to eat. We cook up a real and full feast in the kitchen. When some of the women get sick, we realize we cannot tolerate too much food. Because we lived with less than enough for so long, our bodies are not prepared to handle so much. We talk amongst ourselves about moderation to minimize the sickness. Sick or not, we still celebrate.

The men encourage us to walk about town, even offering to escort us for safety. I get a friend to come with me. I know there can be problems when a girl goes off with a soldier alone. I don't worry much because I am so skinny that no one would be interested in me, but Hiyasura and Yutke both have heard of problems between the women and Russian soldiers.

As we wander freely in the streets, the soldier encourages us, "Take anything you want from the German households, because the Germans are gone. SS soldiers put on civilian clothes and left when they heard we were entering the city."

The soldier explains to us that these are family homes of German soldiers who have gone to war. Their wives and children were left behind to manage on their own. When the families were sure the Russians were coming, they left in fear that the Russians would kill them.

We enter the houses and take food, since food is our main concern. We also take an extra set of clothes to wear. I gather some items for Hiyasura and Yutke as well. We are so joyous as we move about freely, and the soldier watches us with a smile, but he has little insight into how horribly difficult the last year has been. No one can imagine what we endured.

As we walk freely in town with our Russian friend in uniform, I cannot stop smiling. A very unusual feeling comes over my whole body, accompanied by tremendous relief. This is the finest moment of my life. I am 15 years old, and I feel reborn today! I am a whole new person. My mother, three sisters, and little brother did not make it to this moment, so I carry a deep sadness, but nothing can keep me from feeling the sheer joy of freedom. In this moment, I decide to let the other me fade away. I am completely new, free, and alive. It is time to enjoy pure freedom of thought, movement, expression and opportunities. I will never be the same girl I was in Seredne, but I am now a free adult.

Many of the women are sick and very weak when the Russians arrive, so we stay with them for a few weeks until everyone can travel. As time goes on in the company of men, the concern the women have about being raped by Russian soldiers increases. Everyone is grateful when we gain access to travel on trains without needing money. The government allows all displaced persons the opportunity to get home free of charge. Yutke, Hiyasura, and I decide we need to go back to Seredne. We know Momma, Petyu, Blimchu, Fay, Myerbear, and Aunt Lea did not survive, but we are hopeful that Tata and Fischel did. They would know to meet up with us at our house in Seredne.

We are all filled with mixed feelings. Everyone feels liberated and thankful that the war has finally ended, but it is also unpredictable and frightening. There are so many questions. Who is alive? Is there a home to go to? Is there anything left? Why did the world, and God, allow this to happen? I know one thing for sure: we need to go home and hope some other family members are there. All we can do is plan for that.

We begin our journey back to our Seredne, starting at the train station which is overrun with people trying to board the trains. During our three-day wait to get on a train, Hiyasura meets a Czech soldier, named Tibor. They fall in love at the train station. He gives her a key to his apartment in Prague, telling her to stay there while he is in the military. He promises to marry her when he comes back. Hiyasura is so very happy. It is wonderful to see her eyes shine with happiness and love.

The trains only run twice a week, as survivors from all over Europe attempt to get home. The three of us ride on the top of the train because the inside is full. The trip is slow, with stops every 12 miles or so to load and unload passengers. We often change trains to head in the proper direction. The slow progress of the train leaves plenty of time for reflection. I wonder in my mind where was the rest of the world when the Germans were taking us in cattle car trains to Auschwitz? I wonder what it takes for people to help their fellow human beings in the face of adversity? I hope it is much less than a World War.

Now that the war is over, many people change the way they treat Jews. They open their hearts and homes, taking in survivors to sleep for a night. All survivors have access to hostels and eateries free of charge.

After four weeks on the trains, we finally arrive in Seredne and walk to our little farm. Our once beautiful and cozy home is hardly recognizable. The roof is mostly gone, likely from a bomb. All our belongings are gone. They must have housed German horses in it since there is horse manure everywhere. I remember where Tata hid the jewelry, and rush to find it. I am relieved to find the spot is untouched even though the roof is largely gone. I claw at the mud to uncover the shoebox. When my fingers tap a corner of the box, I rapidly remove the mud to extract it, relieved that it remained undiscovered. I climb down to show Yutke and

Hiyasura. We sit down on our kitchen floor and carefully open the lid. Inside is Tata's pocket watch chain, my parents' wedding rings, earrings and a couple of gold chains. All of us cry at the discovery. These are the only things that remain from our past. Tata was so smart to hide the valuables, rather than register them with the Germans! We divide the jewelry amongst the three of us for safekeeping.

Next, we ask neighbors about our furniture and possessions. After going door to door, we quickly see that our neighbors took our furniture, and have no intentions of returning it to us. One man yells, "If you want to live, you better leave. Otherwise we will finish Hitler's job."

I cannot believe these were once our friends, who did business with Tata. Many of these people worked for us before the war. There is no understanding it. It is best to just disregard them and move on.

Since we cannot stay in our home, we stay in town with another survivor who got their home back. Everyone is watching for survivors who return. As the days pass, a few survivors begin to turn up. News travels very quickly when someone arrives. Family members and friends gather to welcome them and ask questions, hoping for news of their loved ones.

One man reported that he knew nothing of Tata but was in a camp with Fischel where they sewed SS uniforms. He described how well my brother did in the camp. Just days before the end of the war, all 300 men in his camp were marched into the forest and were forced to dig a large hole. The Germans then stood them all at the edge of the hole and shot them. As they fell into the hole, it became a mass grave. The man told me that the Germans' goal was to destroy any proof of what they did during the war, so they made sure that there would be no survivors to talk about what happened to them in the camps. I ask the man how he survived, if everyone else died. He tells me that he was too ill to get up, so he hid in the back of the barracks and no one noticed him. As guards walked by his hiding spot later that day, he heard them boasting about their kills to one another. Poor Fischel came within days of liberation, only to be slaughtered by the Nazis. I feel as though cement has filled my heart, hearing about my brother's fate. I think about how close I had been to seeing him again. I could have hugged him one more time if those monsters had not taken him from us. Another soul stolen from our family.

Later, another local man returns with news of our father. This man was with Tata in a factory at Buchenwald, where Tata became very sick. He had sores on his legs that would not heal. Because Tata did not recover and could not work, they shipped him back to Auschwitz where he was murdered. I repeatedly think about him and the injustice, wondering if he was scared. My brave, intelligent father's face swims in my mind. I wonder if he thought of us before he died. I wonder if he felt alone or cried for my mother.

The fate of our immediate family is now clear. Of the 11 Schwartz family members taken, there are only three who survived. Over time we get word of our extended family. Our wonderful family of nearly 150 is reduced to 11 survivors. The town of Seredne also changed. Seredne, Czechoslovakia is now Seredne, occupied Russia or USSR.

After seeing what is left of our home and family, Hiyasura decides to leave for Prague, to Tibor's apartment. I cannot understand why she leaves Yutke and me after Tata said to stay together. But right now, we all need to do whatever we want to make ourselves happy. Yutke and I wave and cry as Hiyasura's train leaves the station. We remain on the platform until the train is out of sight.

Yutke and I stay a few weeks longer in Seredne to relax and recover without worrying. When we attempt to leave on a train, we are denied a ticket. It seems the Russians don't want us to leave. While waiting to get out, Yutke falls in love with a long-time friend from Seredne, named Bumi. He is also a survivor of the war and camps. He is fortunate enough to reclaim his Seredne home. Yutke explains to me with tears in her eyes, that she is tired of not having a home and peace. She wants to settle down and marry Bumi. Again, I see the same look in her eyes that I saw in Hiyasura's and realize I need to honor her wishes. How can I deny her happiness here and insist she leave with me? I understand

Yutke's desire for peace. The war made all of us grow up and deal with harsh realities. In the end, I encourage her to stay with Bumi, giving her a goodbye hug. I decide to go to Prague, to stay with Hiyasura. Yutke and I both know this is not what Tata wanted. We did survive the war following Tata's guidance, but now we need to move apart.

In the end, I convince the ticket master that my whole family is wiped out, except my one sister in Prague. When my tears begin to flow, the guard pauses to consider my situation, then takes pity on me and lets me board the train. Finally, I am leaving for Prague where I can be free. Seredne is no longer my home. It is a thing of the past.

I feel pleasure riding on the train to the city of my choice, in a seat of my choice. It is beautiful to watch the countryside go by for a relaxing week. When I get to Prague, Hiyasura is excited to inform me of an opportunity for orphaned survivor children of the Holocaust, sponsored by the Central British Fund (now World Jewish Relief) in England. I am 16 years old in February of 1946, which makes me eligible for the program. Hiyasura encourages me to go, and not pass up the offer.

Initially I feel uncertain about leaving, but I have no real reason to remain in Prague. Hiyasura assures me that Tata would approve, even though he told us to remain together. She explains the bigger picture to me, the way that Tata used to do. It helps so much to know Tata would want me to get the education and support I need to re-enter the world as an independent woman. Yutke also told me I should get out of Czechoslovakia and the Russian-occupied areas, so that I will know true freedom. Hiyasura is right. I decide to view this opportunity as a new adventure and a way out of a place that has nothing left for me.

Hiyasura and I learn that Leonard Montefiore, a wealthy Jewish philanthropist, and the Central British Fund for German Jewry (CBF) are co-sponsoring a program for 1,000 orphans of the Holocaust. All Holocaust orphans up to the age of 16 are eligible. The plan is to house, treat, educate, and rehabilitate the orphaned refugees in England, Scotland, Ireland and Wales.

Despite the CBF's attempt to gather 1,000 survivor orphans,

they can only locate 732. On February 19, 1946, I join the last transport of survivors to load into Royal Air Force planes. It will be my first plane flight. It is the moment all of us Holocaust orphans dreamed about since being taken. We will fly to Scotland to begin a completely new life. The plane is spacious and cold, and we sit on the floor around the perimeter. They give us blankets. I am both excited and scared. One orphan believes the plane will crash if he shifts his weight to one side, so he stays as still as possible all the way through the long flight. The ride is so bumpy that many of the kids get sick. Everyone is relieved when we land in Prestwick, Scotland. We move through immigration and load buses to Poulton House, in Lasswade, Scotland. Poulton House is a large farm outside of a Scottish village, and the manor house is our hostel. In the previous decade, the house accommodated Jewish refugees from Germany. Some of those refugees return to the farm in 1946 to act as counselors for us kids.

The staff at Poulton House are all Jewish, supportive and loving. It is a real adjustment to realize we are safe and there is enough food every day. No one screams at us, nor threatens our safety. They go out of their way to try to alleviate our fears. Initially, we all worry that this situation isn't real and won't continue. Staff assure us it is real and we can stay until we are ready for the next step.

In this unexpected start to a new life, we have no parents and most of us have no siblings, but we have each other. We all stick together. We become like family. This simple life falls into a pattern of predictable, safe days, which comforts all of us. We are encouraged to have fun and relax together. All of us are eager to feel normal again with our new family.

At Poulton House, we each have our own bed with clean sheets, clothes, and full meals every day. We each have daily chores to care for the house and farm. After chores, mornings are spent in classes at the village school for English, Mathematics, and Geography. School is difficult for me because I don't speak English. I can't understand the teachers and realize I am vastly different from the local students. I missed school in Czechoslovakia for years, and again while in the camps. It feels like I am too far behind to catch up with the rest of the kids. This makes mixing into the public difficult. As a result, many of us usually end up staying together with our survivor-family during school.

Our days are routine and comforting. The counselors talk to us about our new life and what to expect now. We need a long-term plan. They educate us about our options, which include getting support from the United Jewish Federation to possibly emigrate to Palestine. This is not something that interests me, but many of the kids at the manor house consider moving there.

The Small Fortress, Theresienstadt Ghetto Concentration Camp, Terezin, Czechoslovakia

CHAPTER SIX

A Thousand Nights:
Max

In March of 1942, I wake up one morning excited but nervous and a little scared. Today is my Bar Mitzvah, where I will recite the Hebrew prayers just as Dad has carefully taught me. The village synagogue does not have the grandeur of the one we belonged to growing up in Germany, but at least there won't be so many people watching me read the Torah.

Mother lays out our best clothes, as the whole family will celebrate me becoming a man. Today everyone tries to set their worries of the war aside. I look forward to the feast when the service is over that Mother, Grandma and my aunts have been carefully preparing for the last few days.

About three weeks later, an edict is nailed to the trees around the village, that all Jews should report to the nearby ghetto in Zakliczyn. Dad says if we do not follow this edict, our Polish neighbors will round us up and deliver us to the ghetto themselves. My parents want to avoid the ghetto at all costs, but Grandma Schweid and my aunts and uncles follow the orders. We all hug and assure each other that we will reunite soon. I wonder what will happen to them in the ghetto, and what will happen to us staying behind. I think about Grandpa Schindler who must also have to leave his home but has no one to go with him or help him. I don't dare ask Dad what that might mean because he looks so worried right now. I trust Dad to make the right choice for us and believe we will be fine, but am frightened.

Rather than report to the ghetto as ordered, Dad requests a meeting with the administration of the Baeumer Loesch Construction Company, who is organizing a working camp to build roads and bridges. Dad, Fred, I are three able-bodied men who can work. He wants the whole family admitted to the work camp so badly that he bribes the boss to gain access. Mom and Cecilia can help with cooking and cleaning. The Germans accept Dad's personalized, heavy marble desk set that includes a blotter, ink well, pen holders, and a leather case to hold it all. Even though it was one of Dad's favorite things, he looks relieved to hand it over to the Germans to allow us to join the work camp.

Dad tells us not to worry, we will stay together at the work camp and learn skills as we go. In late March of 1942, 100 local Jews, including my immediate family, join Commando Flossenburg in a mainly forced-labor company. Our camp, called Benchashinner, is a small working camp. My brother, Dad and I work together pouring concrete, collecting water underneath the roads, and building a reservoir. I become a fachmann (specialist), working on the roads, building barracks, cutting wood for the bridge and supports for the concrete molds. I am grateful to be working with Dad and Fred each day. Dad has many skills that he shares with us, so we will hopefully stand out as good workers to the Germans.

One day, Fred and I are told to shovel a mountain of coal blocking the railroad tracks. We shovel the coal all day, causing painful blisters on our hands. The next day, we are told to shovel more coal. Our hands are extremely sore but we don't dare complain. Once the guards move away from us, we figure out how to shovel the minimum by putting the shovel handle in our armpit and picking up just one or two pieces of coal at a time. When a guard shows up, we resume shoveling the proper way. As soon as the guard leaves, we again rest our hands. Being caught not working is a serious crime and the guards carry guns. We need to be very careful.

Benchashinner is a self-contained labor camp that is Jewish, but also has local Polish men who work with us during the day. The Poles do not live in camp; they go home at night. The camp is family-style and the members help each other. Everyone agrees that the work camp must be better than what they have heard happens in the ghettos and concentration camps. Here, the men go off to different work sites in the daytime. We do not get paid, but we are also not tortured. We break for lunch with a small meal, then we resume work until it gets dark. The women stay busy cleaning and maintaining the camp, washing and repairing clothes, and taking care of a small garden. Here, everyone wears civilian clothes marked with a Jewish star sewn on their sleeves.

Our group of 100 people become our neighbors, co-workers and friends. Dad says we need to be careful but realize that we all are in the same situation, which gives us things in common. The guards do not interfere when the men get together and pray. It is a comfort for many to have their Bibles and read together.

Like everyone else who has valuables, we sew the few valuables we have into our clothes to conceal them from the German SS officers. Mom and Dad are attached to their wedding rings, and they don't want to lose them. Dad also has a gold pocket watch chain that I keep hidden. The Germans are sometimes aware of the hidden jewelry sewn in clothes, so I keep the chain in my shoe and no one has noticed.

Working on roads is so much harder than farming at Grandma Schweid's, but Fred and I don't complain. Dad reminds us how lucky we are here, compared to what our cousins may be enduring. I am getting steadily stronger from the physical labor. Fred likes working outside with his hands. Dad seems more relaxed lately.

We work side by side with the other men to maintain a calm and reliable system, where the German SS soldiers do not need to keep a close eye on us, except to tell us what our task is each day. They mostly leave us alone.

Almost a year after entering the work camp, in February 1943, we are told that the Commando Flossenburg group is scheduled to evacuate in trucks. We are all surprised to learn that our camp is disbanding and are a little worried. It doesn't take long to gather up our belongings, since we have so few things. Mom assures us it will be all right because we are still together, as she ushers us in the direction the guards lead us. We load onto the trucks without knowing where we are going or what we will be doing when we get there. It looks as though we will remain together with the 100 people who have become like family to us at Benchashinner. They are on the trucks with us. Dad reminds us as he points to each child:

"We will survive, survive, survive!"

The drive is long and bumpy. As the trucks slow down, it is clear this is a different situation than Benchashinner. One of the men hears the guards talking, saying we are in Mielec, Poland. This forced-labor camp is large with long buildings. It is frightening to see people wandering around, looking through us, wearing blue and white striped uniforms. Are we going to become one of them? No one explains what is happening, we're just ordered to move here or move there.

We are taken to a large room where we are told to remove our clothes. I am embarrassed, but notice how deeply uncomfortable the women are. The guards take each piece of clothing we remove and check it for jewelry sewn into the lining, which they proceed to confiscate. Fred, who is in front of me, has some small items sewn into his clothes that a guard finds, tears out and pockets. He tosses Fred's clothes aside, as if they are trash. Fred says nothing. My heart is pounding loudly in my chest now as my turn arrives.

I have Dad's gold watch chain in my pocket, which is very important to me. For some reason, I never sewed it into my clothes, perhaps because I like to see and touch it. All eyes are on me, with the chain held tightly in my hand. Fred makes eye contact with me, and just like when we played kick ball, he knows what I am thinking. He slowly places his hands behind his back and lifts his chin ever so slightly, letting me know that I should put my hands behind my back. While the guards are busy searching my clothes, I place my hands behind my back as Fred slips slowly behind me while he is putting on a blue and white uniform. He takes the chain from me as the guard hands me a uniform and orders me to get dressed. I reach for the uniform with my newly empty hand.

Relief floods over me. Without one word passing between us, the chain is safe with Fred. Clearly this cannot happen again. From now on, I assure myself, we will always be prepared for a search. The watch chain is the only thing we have from our past life and I must find a way to hide it from the Germans. If the chain survives, maybe that means we will survive as well. I return to the present in a jolt when an officer yells at me to get dressed. I then realize it is literally freezing in here.

My striped uniform includes a button-up shirt with long sleeves. There are also long pants with no zipper, just a cord to pull them tighter around my waist. Neither of these is enough to keep me warm in the winter cold. We also each get a pair of wooden clogs that are very uncomfortable and do not keep our feet warm. We have no socks or underclothes of any kind. I never dreamed I would miss my clothes, but I do now. Our clothes are discarded in a pile that is close enough to see, but no longer accessible to any of us.

Soon after donning our blue and white uniform, we enter a long line that moves very slowly. As each person exits the front of the line, I can see them examining their forearm. One man shows us his forearm as he passes us and blurts in Yiddish, "They are tattooing these letters on our arms. How will our God view this?"

He must be an Orthodox Jew. Our faith forbids us to have tattoos. In this moment, I am thankful that we are not Orthodox and were raised to be more relaxed about our faith. I can see the pain on the man's face. Dad assures him, "God would never punish you for something you cannot control."

The tattoo on his forearm says "KL." I intend to find out what that means. So we are waiting in line for a tattoo. I wonder why we need a tattoo here if we didn't need one at the last camp. This new camp is worse than Benchashinner in so many ways already.

Dad and the other men quickly find out from the inmates that KL is shortened from the word konzentrationslager, which means concentration camp. The tattoo identifies us as prisoners of a concentration camp. Dad feared we would end up here. Mom reassures him that our life was manageable at Benchashinner and may be manageable here in Mielec. After all, we survived for many months in the last location. Dad nods affirmatively and says nothing, but the look on his face suggests he may not agree.

Mielec is different in many ways, but the demanding work is the same for us. Dad, Fred and I are assigned to a Heinkel factory that makes aircrafts. Because I am nearly 14 years old and not full-grown, they use me to work inside the airplane wings. I crawl inside and place rivets in the small crevices where other men cannot fit.

We are under constant scrutiny from the armed guards and treated like prisoners here. Our Jewish Flossenburg group works with local Poles who get to go home at night. The Poles hate us and will not help us in any way. At the end of each day, a guard checks everyone's forearms to sort those who stay in camp and those who get to return to their homes. An armed guard then marches the convicts, gypsies and Jews back to the barracks after work.

Here at Mielec, we are separated from Mom and Cecilia at night, which is worrisome. Mom and Cecilia were taken to the women's side of the camp, which we cannot see or visit. It is rare for us to have visual contact or even hear news of them. Fred and I feel very uncomfortable about this, but we keep our worries to ourselves. Dad, who doesn't talk about it, has a permanent crease between his eyebrows now. At least Cecilia has Mom, while Fred and I have Dad.

We sleep in huge barracks where people lay body-to-body on wooden three-tiered bunk beds. I always sleep next to Dad and Fred, as Dad says we are safer together. Every night we lay on straw teeming with lice and bedbugs. There are 300 boys and men per barrack, all of whom suffer the same challenges. The bug bites make it difficult to sleep at night, and in the daytime cause an itchy irritation. In addition, we must wear the same uniform for a month before we get a new one. Getting rid of the bugs is impossible.

Sanitation in the labor camp is awful. There is a cold water trough where we rinse our hands and face. There is no soap. There are no showers. Latrines are pits with a wooden board over them. The board has a round opening for us to squat over, but there is no toilet paper. So many people use the latrine, that it always stinks. Jewish inmates are assigned to clean it. In fact, I realize now that Jews are doing all the work in camp. The guards are just directing them.

I find some tape and mangle Dad's chain into it. The tawny-brown wad in my pocket looks like a small ball of soap. Soap is a prized item here, because no one has access to it. Anyone with soap would guard it carefully, making this the perfect disguise for the gold chain. I keep the watch chain with me always and the disguise proves effective.

Each morning, we get a cup of black coffee for breakfast. It tastes so bad that it makes me want to vomit. I have overheard the men trying to decide what it is made from. Most agree it is comprised of burned oats, wheat, water, and chicory to make it look and smell like coffee. I know I should drink it because I am hungry and thirsty, but I refuse it. Each person carries his own little bowl for food, that attaches to our clothing. At lunchtime, we get a ladleful of soup in this bowl. We sit for a few minutes to drink our soup, then we go back to work in the factory until the end of the day. When we get back to camp, dinner consists of three to four ounces of bread and nothing else. All of us are hungry and thirsty all the time. I see people around me becoming weak and sickly. Everyone is very thin.

Each morning we must show up to be counted. Even when someone is sick, they still must be counted. Dad, Fred, and I help each other and our barrack mates stand-up if we feel too weak, to prevent any consequences with the German soldiers. They are harsh and unpredictable. The smallest thing can send them into a rage and people are shot. After the counting, we go back to the barracks and wait until the SS call us. Waiting gives us a chance to rest, sometimes for up to two hours. Everyone in the camp is weak and malnourished, but we go on to work no matter what. Everyone knows prisoners who cannot work are shot or sent to the gas chamber.

When something breaks in the women's area, one of the men is assigned to fix it. The worker always searches for family and asks for news when they are on that side of the camp and share with the women news of their men. Upon the worker's return, the worried men get an update. It is not unusual to hear, "No one has seen her lately." This can mean many things, including death. At least this concentration camp does not have a crematorium to incinerate prisoners as we have heard other camps do.

In January, 1944, it has been nearly a year of work in the airplane factory, and the camp is less full. We have all noticed steadily decreasing numbers of inmates. We wonder what will happen next. Are the Allies coming to liberate us? Are we going to move to another camp? No one knows, and concern is building because change usually means more hardship for us.

We are relieved when our new orders finally come. The German officers command us to dismantle the aircraft factory. We will move the factory to another location. The rumor around the camp is that the Allied forces are getting close, and the Germans don't want any evidence of their exploits to remain.

Early in February of 1944, the Commando Flossenburg group is scheduled to move by train. The German SS tell us the move is for our safety because the Russians are reportedly nearby. We do not want to be in the middle of an armed conflict, as we could all be killed. Our lives have been threatened so many times at this point that I feel a little numb to this threat. We set forth dismantling the entire factory, and load all the machinery onto a train. The dismantling and transporting task takes several days. When everything is done, the train pulls out of the station with the Heinkel factory essentials and inmates on board. We travel to Wieliczka, Poland, which is near Kraków, with a contingent of armed German guards watching us.

Once we arrive in Wieliczka, we follow orders to unload all

the equipment and transport it into the salt mines, where it is less likely to be found by enemy troops. It is a tremendous job to move all the heavy equipment from the train into the salt mines. We are all extremely weak and very tired but keep working as steadily as we can.

Very soon after moving here, we notice a problem. The metal machinery reacts to the salt and begins corroding and rusting. We are not even fully reconstructed when the Germans realize the salt mine is a bad choice because of the reaction on the metal. The machinery will rust and freeze up if it remains in the mine. We know the Germans made a huge mistake but say nothing. There are murmurings about why the Germans would make such a poor decision. Were they rushing? Regardless of why they chose this location, no manufacturing can happen here. Within days, we follow orders, yet again, to dismantle the factory.

During the time in Wieliczka, we do not see Mom or Cecilia at all and become very concerned. After using our clandestine communication system among the prisoners, we learn that the women did not come to Wieliczka. Instead, they were sent to Plaszow. SS officers tell us Plaszow is nearby. It is our next destination since this location is not serviceable, so we will hopefully see Mom and Cecilia soon. This is some consolation, but nothing will truly comfort us until we actually see them. We cannot leave the salt mines fast enough, and this makes the drudgery of disassembling the equipment and loading it back on the train less difficult. Our intent is to get to Plaszow so all of our Flossenburg families can be reunited.

As soon as everything is stowed, we are eager to leave but try not to show it. We finally arrive at the Plaszow concentration camp late in February of 1944. We go through all of the routine checks which we now know how to manage, but not without concern for the gold chain that I continue to hide and carry with me. I have observed that the officers rarely check shoes when inmates arrive from other camps. We no longer have personal clothes and the officers seem less concerned that we might still have something of value, so they are less thorough with their checks. No one knows about the chain, except Fred.

Plaszow is another concentration camp with brutal guards, disgusting and minimal food, packed sleeping quarters, and lack of hygiene. These things are not important to us now. Our goal is to locate Mom and Cecilia. Despite going through all the back channels of inside communication among inmates, we cannot find out any information on Rachela or Cecilia Schindler. Dad, Fred and I are very anxious and try not to fear the worst. The rumor in camp is that the Russians are now close to Warsaw and are threatening to override the Germans. The Allies are coming. Poland and Germany are bracing for attack. The soldiers here are more tense than at the other camps. We need to be very careful not to test their patience, because they become more explosive with very little provocation now.

At this camp, we do not work in a factory. Instead, we move around the city of Kraków to dig ditches and build fortifications for the German troops. We are also forced to begin the work of dismantling the concentration camp at Plaszow, so there will be no evidence of what has transpired here. Clearly, the Germans are worried about the opposition closing in on them as they are trying to hide the atrocities they inflicted in the concentration camps. They want it to look like the camps never even existed. We have to survive so we can tell the world what really happened.

It is rainy and cold in the late winter, and we are standing in the mud all day long. I feel truly miserable. These circumstances prove to be too much for some men. As a result, a few inmates try to escape, using the ditches we dug to try to get away. The Germans capture these prisoners and decide to make an example of them for the rest of us. The dead bodies of our co-workers who tried to escape hang listlessly on wooden poles where we walk to go to the bathroom or line up to be counted. The circumstances could not be worse, I think. All of us are so tired, starving and feeling almost hopeless.

Work continues no matter what. People who can't work are sent to Auschwitz to be gassed. All inmates, including the Flossenburg group, are disassembling the Plaszow concentration camp. When the work is complete, we realize we must move again. In our whole stay at Plaszow, there is no news of Mom and Cecilia. The camp is closing, we are leaving, and we have not seen them for a very long time. As we prisoners load onto cattle cars to ride the rails to the next camp, I have a sick feeling in my stomach.

The train fills with inmates yet again and shuttles around for two days. At times, it heads toward Auschwitz, meaning certain death for all of us. Many people feel sure that is our destination. Each time the train heads in that direction, prisoners cry out and sob. After a time, the train veers in a different direction, giving people hope again and the sobbing stops. Darkness, exhaustion, no food, and no water leaves each man less than himself. Everyone is near the edge of their ability to cope. Dad, Fred and I keep encouraging each other at various times, repeating the mantra, "Don't listen to the worries, just survive, survive, survive."

In the end, Auschwitz is not our destination. The train comes to rest in Zschachwitz, near Dresden. It is March of 1944 and 300 of us arrive at the next factory to work. We build tanks alongside Germans who get to go home at night. We do not interact with the German workers, except when our job tasks overlap. I again become a fachmann (specialist) and work the drill press.

While our housing is better than a barrack and has modern conveniences, the situation is frightening because we are housed with criminals. The three-story building contains a factory and a bomb shelter. Jews sleep on the top floor. We all know a man's alleged crime by the triangle patch he wears on his uniform. Each color denotes a different crime: convicted criminal is green; political prisoner is red; foreign laborer is blue; homosexual or rapist is pink; kidnappers, mentally ill, alcoholics, or beggars are black; Jehovah's Witnesses are purple. Our insignia remains the yellow Star of David. Dad advises us to avoid being alone in the residence, and to not engage with any of the prisoners at all. We are to assume they are all dangerous.

I think about the gold watch chain, worried that if a criminal knows I have it, he will kill me for it. Dad's gold watch chain has survived many inspections between my brother and me, in a hand, in a pocket, or a wooden clog, passed wordlessly back and forth between us. The chain is more important to us now because it has survived with us despite the odds. We both somehow believe if it survives, then we will, as well.

The food here is better than camp, but still not enough to sustain us. Men are weak and thin, sickly and have difficulty completing their jobs. There is a civilian German man here, the only one in all the places I have been during the war, who feels any concern for me. He sneaks me bread from his home. I hide it at work, then share with Dad and Fred in the residence. It melts in my mouth. I want to gobble it down, like when I took fresh bread for granted on the farm, but savor it one small pinch at a time.

This man is putting his life and mine at risk by giving me bread. We are very careful that no guards are watching when he hands it to me. I am dumbfounded by his courage and kindness.

At the factory, each of us has a station where we work 10 hours a day, every day. Here I am at 14 years old, a drill press operator. Water flows into my drill press from an attached tank to keep it from overheating. The tank is smaller than a bale of hay. The water in the tank is somewhat yellowish, which gives me an idea. I wonder if I can hide my gold chain in the tank? The chain is the same color as the tank water. I feel certain no one will look in it for hidden items, but it is imperative that no one sees me hiding it.

I carefully check to be sure no one is watching, roll up my sleeves and plunge my fist into the water letting the gold chain slip through my fingers. We are in such close quarters, I feel scared. But no one notices. The chain is invisible in the tank and can remain there for as long as necessary. I am relieved to have found a safe place for it, hidden away from the guards and the criminals that I live with.

We remain at this location for nearly a year. Our work in the factory is consistent and comfortingly predictable. We hear with increasing frequency from the grapevine that the Allies are closer. Even some of the local Germans talk about what will happen if the Allies enter Dresden.

The night of February 13, 1945 the Allies' saturation bombing of Dresden begins. The sky lights up with flares from the first wave of planes. Subsequent waves of bombers drop phosphorous bombs that cause fires after exploding. The entire city has become a giant torch. When our factory housing gets hit, fire spreads quickly. Pandemonium breaks out as we prisoners run down the stairs to the bomb shelter. In the confusion of masses moving quickly, a pileup of bodies snags Fred and he gets trapped. Dad and I frantically struggle to free him from the human pile. We pull and push body parts, when suddenly Fred lets out a short scream as he breaks free. He has lost a shoe and his foot is bleeding as we haul him upright and help him down the stairs. My fears begin to subside as we descend to the bomb shelter, with Fred hopping on one foot. The words "survive, survive, survive" repeat in my head like a comforting chant.

Once we arrive at the bomb shelter, we examine Fred's foot. Using our shirts to soak up the blood, we realize he lost a toe nail in the mayhem. Although it is painful, he knows he is very lucky, as some men died in the pileup on the stairs.

Two days later the bombing is finally over. When we crawl out of the bomb shelter, we see that the factory is half gone, and the accommodations upstairs for the inmates is lost. We must now sleep with no roof. It is literally freezing temperatures and we have no blankets. We can see from the top floor of our bombed-out building local people roaming in the streets, lost in the city. People push their belongings in carts and baby carriages, with nowhere to go. Dad, Fred and I discuss our options and plan to escape. However, if we do, we will have nowhere to sleep, no food to eat, or means of transport out, so we decide instead to wait for liberation. We can hear the bombs exploding in the distance, and know the Allies are approaching.

During all the commotion, I realize I left the watch chain in the drill press. I discuss it with Fred and we devise a plan to retrieve it. Fred watches for people in one direction, and I watch the other. When the coast is clear, I run back into the factory. I find my machine and open the water storage tank, reaching in blindly to feel for the wadded-up chain. It is there and in my hand! I feel a rush of relief and hear the words, "Just survive, survive, survive." Grabbing the chain, I run as fast as I can back to Fred and Dad. No one even noticed me going back into the factory!

After a few days, the German SS soldiers, with guns on their shoulders, round up the Commando Flossenburg group again and we set off on a forced march. We are 300 to 350 men marching through the forest, into Czechoslovakia. The march takes a few weeks but feels more like a year, and is ghastly for our group. We march on one side of the river, watching bombs explode on the other side. With snow on the ground, all of us are freezing, as we climb up into the mountains. I can't feel my toes and try to walk with my hands tucked into my armpits. We get very little to eat, and we are all starving. We march through several towns as people stand by the side of the road and silently watch. We are told not to speak to townspeople or accept anything from them, or else we will be shot. Not one person offers us anything. No food or jackets or boots or blankets. It is a disastrous death-march from bombed-out Dresden to Litomerice. I see men fall, give up and die, or sit down and refuse to go on. These people are all shot. Dad's health declines and he is in bad shape. He is very weak and cannot walk alone. Fred and I support him on either side with his arms over our shoulders. When we get tired after hours of assisting him, other men from our group help hold him up.

The Germans stuff us in a barn in a subcamp called Litomerice our first two nights after the death march. At long last, we are given a small amount of food, which is our first food in 8 to 10 days. We sleep on the dirt floors squashed together to try to stay warm, our first night's sleep in almost 10 days. No one cares about the abhorrent conditions as we are completely exhausted and barely alive! Two days later, when we arrive at Theresienstadt Ghetto (concentration camp) in late March of 1945, there are only about 80 of our group who are still alive after the forced death march. The rest are dead.

At some point, we learn Jewish prisoners continue to arrive daily at Theresienstadt by every possible method of transport: train, truck, and forced death marches. Prisoners from all over German-occupied Europe arrive as other camps close, without concern for this camp's capacity. Everyone is near death, completely exhausted and starving. The camp is over-crowded, filthy and disorganized. The next morning we are marched under guard to the Small Fortress, which is about a half-mile outside Theresienstadt's wall, as there is no room for us inside Theresienstadt Ghetto. The plan to move so many prisoners here was not well thought out. Fred and I secretly think the Germans know their days are numbered.

In the Small Fortress, Jewish Kapos notice that our dad is in desperate need of immediate medical attention. The Kapos take him to a room called the hospital room where they hold the sickest Jewish prisoners, who receive no medical attention or food. The hospital room is under quarantine. Emancipated Jewish men lay dying on the floor around the perimeter of the room. I can see Dad through a barred window but am not allowed into the room due to the quarantine. Fred and I stop at the window where Dad is when we can find the strength, which gets harder every day. Each time we stop at the window to see him, we hope he regains consciousness so we can catch his attention, to reassure him we are still alive. Once or twice Dad and I lock eyes and acknowledge each other. There is so much that goes unsaid but is understood in those moments. I'm hoping and praying that Dad will pull through and survive.

Fred, Dad and I remain in the Small Fortress for one to two weeks with little-to-no food. It is very scary here. The Small Fortress has been used as a prison and human torture site for many decades. It is now springtime and the rainy season, so the floors we sleep on are muddy. It is very cold and uncomfortable, but we are determined to survive. Eventually we are transfered to the Theresienstadt Ghetto for the duration of the war, trying to stay alive while hearing the sounds of war and fighting approaching.

On May 8, 1945, Soviet troops enter Theresienstadt and the Small Fortress to liberate the camps! Could this be the day we have waited so long for? The troops are, indeed, here to liberate us! Our imprisonment at the hands of the Germans is over at last! Even the weakest of us is celebrating to know we are finally, finally free. We did survive! We are no longer captives, prisoners and slaves to the German Nazis. The three of us, despite all the odds, have survived to today's liberation, although Dad is very likely at death's door. I can now proudly wear Dad's gold watch chain, rather than hide it.

Fred is in better shape than I am. I cannot get up. Realizing that we are free men, Fred decides to walk out to the nearest village in search of food. Within a few hours, he brings back a can of sardines, which we haven't seen in years. Both of us are eager to try some. He opens the can and we each eat a couple sardines. The salty fish taste is overpowering but feels strangely nourishing. It has been so long since we have eaten real food. It tastes delicious but I am too exhausted to eat more than a couple of bites.

The day after liberation, on May 9, 1945, Germany surrenders to the Allies and the war in Europe is ended. That day we both become very ill due to epidemic typhus, like most of the survivors in Theresienstadt and the Small Fortress. The Americans arrive that day, bringing with them the Red Cross, who quickly sets up makeshift hospital triage rooms to care for us. Typhus causes a very high fever and I become delirious. Once I regain some of my awareness (I have no recollection how long I was out), I realize we are still in the Small Fortress. Fred and I are in improvised hospital beds covered with white sheets.

I am not sure I didn't dream this. White sheets? How can that be? I haven't seen a bed sheet in years. Again, I wake up and this time ask the Red Cross nurse, who confirms that Fred and I are in a makeshift hospital in isolation with epidemic typhus. Immediately after liberation, the entire camp came down with typhus's high fever and many who had survived to this point died over the last couple weeks. Our fever continues and we remain in isolation for many days or weeks. I fear I might not survive this illness. I somehow believe I cannot be trusted to watch over the gold chain any longer. I am so weak that it takes all my energy to stand up and walk over to over Fred in a nearby bed, and fasten the chain around his neck. I whisper in his ear, "You have it. You take care of it now."

Fred wears the chain proudly as we convalesce.

At the end of many weeks in the makeshift hospital, the quarantine lifts on July 13, 1945. We have been awake and alert for some time but need to complete the quarantine before they let us leave. Fred is wearing the gold chain now. It speaks volumes to both of us of what we endured, and how we never quit. Occasionally, I see Fred touching the chain, lost in thought. Fred and I know we need to find Dad, who must be terribly worried and wondering where we are. As the days in quarantine pass, our concern grows for him. What will he think became of us? Has he recovered from his illness?

When we are finally released, Fred and I cannot get out of the quarantine soon enough. We both hurry as fast as we can to the hospital to check on Dad. We arrive at the window breathing heavily, but we do not see him. We begin searching other windows to see if they moved him. He is not in any of the beds. Fred remains at the window where we last saw him, waving at staff to get their attention while I go to the door and insist that I need help locating my dad. I ask everyone I can for information on his whereabouts, from nurses to orderlies. No one knows anything, but Dad is definitely not at the hospital. There are no patient records. Most were so sick they couldn't talk or didn't know their own names. All came without any identifying documents on them. Dad's only identifying information on admission to this temporary hospital was his KL tattoo that marked him as a survivor of the concentration camp. He would not have left this place without us. We never separated in three and a half years of difficulty and unpredictable events.

We slowly come to the realization that Dad did not survive the typhus epidemic. Fred and I share a long, knowing look. We both know. I can see it in his eyes: Benjamin Schindler is dead. After a quiet period, we begin talking about what likely happened. I hope that Dad lived long enough to know liberation. Fred believes this is true. He hopes that Dad did not worry about us too much. After another long pause, I suggest maybe Dad thought we died, so he gave up the fight. There are so many thoughts and emotions to sort through. This will take time. We have the rest of our lives to figure out this piece. For now, we need to decide what is the next step for us.

Now that our long-held, quiet dream of "just survive" is real, we are confused. What should we do next? Where are Mom and Cecilia? Should we go back to Germany? I, for one, no longer feel like "a German first and a Jew second," as Dad used to say. I want nothing to do with Germans. Fred and I just spent over three years in forced labor and concentration camps as slaves to them. I blame the Germans for Dad's death. I am sure he survived to liberation but did not have the strength left in him to remain with us. Right now, I need to find my Mom and sister, then a new home.

After liberation, people wander around looking confused, relieved, and angry and all have questions about their loved ones. There are many groups trying to help the survivors. United Nations Relief and Rehabilitation Administration (UNRRA), the Red Cross, and the Jewish Committee all are present. The Red Cross tries to locate family members in camps to reconnect, or to validate their deaths. People are searching for lost family, taking trains home, and going to new destinations.

With the help of the Red Cross, we find out that Mom and Cecilia went to Stutthof, a camp in East Prussia. That concentration camp reportedly expanded several times, adding more barracks and extermination chambers during the war. They tell us Rachela and Cecilia Schindler were killed there. Just before liberation, all surviving Stutthof inmates were loaded onto barges, pushed out into the Baltic Sea and were deliberately sunk. Our worst fear is realized. We worried about Mom and Cecilia's safety every day we were suffering in the camps, keeping hope alive that they would survive. Learning with certainty that they are dead is a tremendous blow.

The Red Cross also investigated our family in Poland that went to the ghetto at Zakliczyn. They tell us that our cousins, aunts, uncles and Grandma Schweid were all killed. None of them survived. We also find out that our dear Grandpa Schindler refused to go to a ghetto when the Jews were rounded up in Brzesko in 1942. He was shot in the street near his home. At 90 years old, he refused to leave his home. We now know our whole family is gone, murdered by the German Nazis.

Dad is dead. Mom and Cecilia are gone. Our extended family no longer exists. It is just Fred and me in the world. All that remains from our former life is the gold chain that Dad wore to hold his watch. Both of us need time to process this information and develop a plan. Fred and I feel as lost as so many of the people wandering around us.

For a few days, we watch what others are doing. Thousands

of people board trains to go home. It is strange to see them come back to Theresienstadt where we are. They report a variety of terrible things. Some find no other family survived, their homes are now lived in by strangers or are emptied of all goods; some are harassed and threatened. All those who returned, recommend that liberated Jews are better off not going home, particularly if their homeland is Poland. They warn us to leave Poland, for our own safety. We hear reports of brutal murders of liberated Jews trying to return home. The next question is: if not Poland, and certainly not Germany, then where do we go?

The UNRRA relief workers inform us about one group of survivors going to Palestine and a second group going to England. We remember our family talking about going to Palestine. We know that there is the possibility of a war brewing for Jews to have their own place in Palestine. Neither of us are interested in participating in another war, even if it is for a just cause. This, and our view of America as free, progressive, and a land of opportunity, leads us toward the group going to England. From England we may be able to reach the United States. Dad wanted to get our family to America but had been unable to finalize the paperwork as the war closed in on us.

Relief workers inform us that the English will support us, help us learn skills to survive in the world, and give us medical and emotional care. This sounds infinitely better than fighting a war for freedom. England, and the support it offers, seems like our best option.

The relief workers tell us an English philanthropist named Leonard Montefiore saw concentration camp survivors in Paris while he was visiting and was moved to help them. He never forgot the "walking corpses with sunken eyes and parchment skin." Montefiore wanted to do something for them. He worked with the English government to develop a plan to help orphaned Holocaust children survivors. English regulations prevent money being sent to the survivors in their home country, when the government is involved. Instead, the English can give support by bringing orphaned survivors under the age of 16 to England for rehabilitation.

Fred and I learn that the goal of the Central British Fund for German Jewry and Mr. Montefiore is to bring 1,000 Jewish child orphaned survivors to the United Kingdom for rehabilitation. Fred and I like the idea of joining the English group, but we have a problem. The maximum age for entering the group is 16. Fred is 17.

None of us survivors have a birth certificate or any identifying documentation. We left our homes in haste, and everything we brought with us was confiscated. Because we don't have any form of identification, we need a system to get some. The support staff, in conjunction with the Czech government, help survivors obtain new documents. Fred and I quietly agree to lie about our ages. We are in luck because the aid workers are aware of our predicament, but help us and several other kids modify their ages to make it possible to join the group. Like many survivor orphans, we have nowhere else to go and no one to go home to, so they believe it is the least they can do to help us.

The permis de sejour (temporary visitor visa) allows us to enter Great Britain and remain for five years for rehabilitation. After this time, we must emigrate on. This document will serve as our new birth certificate. The document requires us to identify a final destination, at the end of the five years as a visitor. Most of the kids choose Palestine. Fred and I also choose Palestine. With our new birth certificates, Fred is 16 and I am 15. Fred and I are accepted in the group, along with other orphan child survivors. The survivors, nicknamed "The Boys," include girls as well. The group grows, reaching a total of 732 kids. The Red Cross Commission completes a physical on each of us and decides if we are healthy enough to travel to the United Kingdom. Fred and I both pass the examination and prepare to go to England on Royal Air Force transport airplanes.

First group of "The Boys" survivors in Prague Town Square, Prague, Czechoslovakia, August 1945

CHAPTER SEVEN

Finally, Freedom from Camps:
Max

We move by train from Theresienstadt to Prague on August 11, 1945. We are told that we will remain in Prague until transport to the United Kingdom is secured. Going to England is a grand dream, and most of us cannot believe it is actually happening. This train is no cattle car. We have a seat, a bathroom, water, and food. During the train ride, we have time to reflect on many things. We can move freely about, talk and play. No one is patrolling us with guns on their shoulders.

In Prague, we move into clean youth hostels where we each have a our own bed with fresh linens, large meals and warm showers. Freedom means we can now move about as we please, speak without having to whisper so no guard will overhear, and choose what we want to do. We do not work from sun up to sundown, enduring guards who may shoot us for any small infraction. We eat enough food at every meal, every day. I have lived with fear of not having enough food for nearly four years. It is hard to get used to the plentiful food that won't disappear again. I can walk freely with friends around the city. Fred and I make the most of this, going to movies, where we are admitted free of charge. We watch American, English, and Czech movies. It is a great escape from the life we lived for all those years. We always sit in the first row and feel like we are living it up a little. Local bakeries treat us to cakes every afternoon. They taste incredible, better than anything I can remember.

When our long-awaited day to start a whole new life in England arrives, Fred and I are excited beyond words... and not quite sure this isn't all a dream. We are excited to go but also feel a little sad to leave Prague because the people have been so kind and generous to us. On the other hand, I cannot wait to get away from all the places and unspeakable things we endured during the war.

We load onto the train in disbelief that we are really leaving. When the brief ride comes to an end near the airport, we walk a short distance to the Belgitska Street Hostel. The counselors tell us we need to remain here until a storm clears that has halted all airplane travel. We stay at the hostel for three days, feeling discouraged. Our organizers reassure us that we are definitely going to England, but not in this storm. They want to be sure we arrive safely.

Counselors explain that there are many hurdles to get us orphans to England, including the weather. The Ministry of the Interior in Prague plans to use planes that bring Czech Air Force soldiers home from England, now that their service is complete. They tell us once the Air Force troops deplane, we will board for the flight back to England. Leonard Montefiore and his Committee for the Care of Children from Concentration Camps (CCCCC) work closely with the Central British Fund to meet all of our needs when we arrive.

When ten Royal Air Force Lancaster bombers are ready at Ruzyne airport, we load onto buses for the short trip to the airport. The moment we have dreamed of is really going to happen. The excitement amongst us is palpable. None of us has ever been on an airplane before, or been to England. As we exit the buses onto the tarmac, there is time for a photo of the group just before we board. Our group of 300 survivors is separated into smaller groups. The pilots call us "precious cargo." We climb into the belly of the plane and sit on the floor lined up along the edges. As we gain altitude, the air inside the plane gets colder. We huddle in the blankets they provided, but we are still freezing cold. Since there are no bombs needed for this flight, the bomb bay door remains open. Fred and I can see land and water through the bomb bays. It feels like we are on an exciting, scary and rocky boat ride.

Our flight makes a stop in Wales, where they serve us tea on the tarmac while the airplane gets refueled. When the plane is ready again, we reload and continue our journey to Crosby-on-Eden airport in Lancaster, England. Mr. Montefiore and several other officials greet each of us individually. He tells us he is genuinely pleased to see us in England. We board buses and head to Windermere, an unused aircraft factory. The staff tell us that we will love being here, in the idyllic lake district. They serve us hot cocoa and white bread. I have never seen or tasted white bread before, since we always ate rye bread growing up. I think the white bread is cake, and decide that this is going to be a wonderful life, where they feed us cake everyday.

At Windermere, we are warmly greeted and are told we are welcome here. We each get a room with a bed, blanket, pillow, clean sheets, and a dresser. A place of my own? Truly my own room and belongings? This really is a dream come true.

We still are in the habit of worrying about food at each meal, but there seems to be more than we need every day. When I talk to Fred and the others, we are in awe and wonderment at this wonderful, safe place and its kind people. It is hard to believe it will continue.

The first several weeks we are in quarantine, a controlled environment, as many of the kids are sick. The doctors explain that we are still carriers of tuberculosis which I contracted in Theresienstadt. The medical staff want to be sure we are not contagious before sending us out into the local community. Windermere is clean, there is plenty of food and the people are so kind to us that we don't mind being in quarantine. This place has white sheets and white bread. It must be heaven.

All of the staff at Windermere are Jewish and quite concerned with the well-being of us survivors. Oscar Friedman, an orphan and pre-war refugee himself, is instrumental in leading our rehabilitation. As the madrich (counselor) for the group, he is a devoted guide whose policy is to minimize rules, feed our desire to learn and allow us as much social freedom as possible.

Mr. Montefiore knows that we survived the "greatest human-made Hell in history," and need extra psychological help to recover. Oscar steps up to the task, making our mental health his number one priority. Berish Lerner visits each boy at his bedside the first night and speaks to us in fluent Yiddish, establishing a deep bond as one of our own. He has a similar background to us and connects immediately. A close relationship and trust builds amongst the staff and kids, and fear slowly wanes. Over time, counselors begin reintroducing us to our faith. It is a delicate task, for which there is no guide book of instructions to follow. Faith is hard to embrace for many, after what we all endured.

Windermere is meant to stabilize us medically, then disperse survivors to the many locations throughout the UK that are staffed by volunteers. Once we are medically cleared, we begin to leave Windermere in groups of 30 to 35. We don't know when we will see each other again, but know we are headed in the right direction. There is a large part of our lives that we want to leave behind and this is one step. We disperse to 24 different hostels throughout England, Scotland, Wales, and Northern Ireland that can accommodate groups of orphans. These hostels are staffed largely by German Jews who were refugees housed in England before the war. These volunteers were originally called the "children's transports." There are also English people who want to help.

When we are finally cleared by the doctors, Fred and I move to Alton, a village in England. The hostel there provides everything we need. The instructors and counselors tell us that they hope to build our physical and spiritual health, education, confidence and social skills. They also want each of us to eventually have a job skill, so we can become independent in the world. We attend Organization for Rehabilitation and Training School for half a day, five days a week. This school is designed to prepare us for life and work. The leaders at each location are devoted to us and we are so appreciative of their attention. Here we have time to relax, learn and play. We feel happy. Some of us don't remember what it was like to be happy, but all of us over time, learn to enjoy our new life.

Part of being at the hostel is participating in the care and maintenance of the building. We all have chores to do, to keep the place running. It is nothing like the demanding work we had in the camps, so we do our chores without complaint. In some ways, our chores remind many of us of life at home before the war. There is a predictability and resemblance of normalcy in performing the chores.

Every other week we have a physical exam to be sure we maintain or improve our health. Fred and I are both feeling much better, except for one thing. Fred's hair is falling out, which seems odd to us. No one in our family had baldness. It is not a big concern and the doctors don't seem worried, so we don't make a big deal of it. The doctors help Fred get a wig which looks nice on him.

Sports teams start up and we are encouraged to join in. Fred, who likes sports, joins willingly. We are told the activities will help us regain our strength and learn life lessons as a group. There is soccer, volleyball, swimming and bike riding. I am not a sports enthusiast like Fred, but I do enjoy the sense of freedom while bike riding around anywhere I choose to go.

One teacher teaches metal crafts. I decide to join this group and really enjoy the fabrication process and learning how to handle the tools. We begin by making small useful items like ashtrays, and gradually progress to lamps and wrought iron tables. Our teacher uses English more and more in the shop to help us learn the language. We also learn English during our half-day schooling on-site, at the hostel.

Fred and I remain at Alton for a year and fall into a stable and predictable routine of classes, activities that we choose, and rest. We can ride bikes into town, play in the lakes, or relax and read a book. The harsh environment and work of the camps is behind us now. Over time, however, the counselors encourage us to think of a trade we want to learn. The time is coming when we will need to support ourselves in the world.

In late 1946, Fred and I relocate to another hostel in Bedford, England. We again find very supportive staff, safe lodging, and plenty of food. The residents are like a very big family that is growing into a new lifestyle together. The counselors tell us that we did not deserve the suffering that we endured, that it cannot stop us now, and we can be anything we want to be if we are willing to work hard. They also encourage us to help each other and establish friendships.

Some of the orphans still plan to go to Palestine. The hostel teachers and counselors encourage survivors to make this transition. Those who choose to move to Palestine are paired with young families in England who live on farms. The farmers teach the survivors farming techniques to prepare for life in Palestine. Many of these boys immigrate to Palestine in late 1947 and 1948. Fred and I are sure this is not for us. We will stay in England to learn a trade and master English, with the thought of eventually going to Palestine or locating relatives in the U.S. who can sponsor us to emigrate there.

During this time period, we hear news from Scotland that the Poulton House is beginning to clear out since so many survivors are leaving for Palestine, Australia, Canada, and the United States. They are moving the rest of the orphans here to Bedford so we can all be together. I am unsure what to think about how this will affect us, but it will be nice to meet new people who understand me.

Rose with her friends from "The Boys" survivors in Lasswade, Scotland, 1946

CHAPTER EIGHT

Trying for Normal:
Rose

Our Scottish hostel is quickly emptying as more and more girls move on to Palestine (soon to become Israel). I think long and hard about going with them, but ultimately, I decide that England has many more opportunities for me. A few days later, they tell us that we will be moved to a place called Bedford, where other survivors are housed. Many are nervous to move, but I think it is a wonderful opportunity to grow and experience a new country. I am happy to go on another adventure.

We make the long journey by train to Bedford where a group of counselors welcomes us to the hostel. I look around and can't help noticing that the five of us women who came from Scotland are the only women who will be staying at the Bedford hostel. I learn at the orientation that Bedford housed only male refugees up until now. The hostels are combining groups of survivors as many move on to other destinations. New rules are established regarding how males and females will interact now that we live in the same hostel.

One young man in the group catches my eye. He is the most handsome young man at Bedford with his wavy brown hair. He is reserved and refined, compared to the rest of the men. When he smiles at me, I smile back. Slowly he and another man walk towards my friends Berta, Cecilia and me.

"Hello, I am Max and this is my brother Fred," he says. "Welcome to Bedford."

Understanding very little English at this point, he gestures to himself so I can figure out what he means. I smile and nod at him.

When they walk off, I tell Berta that I think they are nice men. She agrees that the one called Max is very handsome. We are careful around the men, because we are not to fraternize with them. This is part of the agreement we signed in allowing us to move here, since there are so many men and only five women. I try to follow the rules, but Max made an impression on me.

In the following days we are told that we are family now, and that we should treat each other as such. This group is meant to help us all practice becoming "normal" again. We do not speak of the horrors of the camps to each other much. Everyone wants to put that aside and begin anew. I feel connected with the young women, but it is hard for me to connect with the men. They don't feel like brothers. I feel like I must keep myself apart because of the rules we need to follow here.

We are all from many different countries. When I walk down the hall, I frequently hear many languages being spoken. English is still difficult for me, but it is a little easier to understand than the Scottish/English accent we heard in Scotland. A counselor tells me that the Scottish accent is very strong and that may be why I struggled to pick up English. Even though I can speak six other languages, I realize that I need to learn English to be able to interact with others, get a job, and start a new independent life.

Fred and Max in England, 1946

CHAPTER NINE

Claiming Independence:
Max

The new survivors from Scotland are hard to understand. Fred and I have nicknamed them the "Don't Touch Me" girls, but there is something about them that fascinates me. When together, they seem to laugh and interact normally with one another, but when a man enters the room, they all clam up and sit quietly. I don't understand why they won't talk to us. I didn't have any trouble talking to my sister at home. These girls are different and don't feel like family at all. I know we are to treat each other as family and learn to be "normal" again, so I will be patient.

At first, I think they might be scared, but Fred says he thinks it's about how they were raised. He talks with a counselor who says that women from their areas are taught to be demure and quiet. Right now, it is not a problem because we don't speak the same language anyway, but it would be nice to get to know them once they learn more English. I tried to speak with them in German, but they do not know it. They tried to speak to me in a number of different languages, including Yiddish which most of the men here speak, but I never learned it. So, for now, I can't speak to them. I can only look at them.

Soon after the girls arrive, I find a job at a local foundry making metal castings. It is close enough that I can ride my bike to and from work every day, which gives me a chance to see a little bit of the country. I appreciate this because the foundry work is all indoors. We have to run the fire all day to melt down the metal, which means that I am always hot and tired. First, it has to get roaring hot. Then I melt the metal and pour it into a form, where it cools and hardens into a new shape. I feel like I am in a sweatshop. I am happy to have work, but I dislike this kind. One night I talk to Fred about it, and he says that I should find work that I like. I tell him that I know and like woodworking, so maybe I can find work as a carpenter. He agrees that this would be a better choice for me, and with my prior experience, I could probably find a new job easily.

After work the next day, I start searching for a new job that will allow me to use my woodworking skills. That night, I feel happier as I bike home from my job search. I know that soon my foundry days will be over. It takes a few weeks, but eventually I find work at a truck-repair factory. I quit my job at the foundry and become a woodworker at the factory, repairing old trucks and building new, more modern wooden bodies for truck frames.

One day, I am working on a particularly stubborn part, when I notice a truck pull up to the open door of the factory. Men jump down off the truck bed and head up to the office area. Initially I think nothing of this, but when I hear the German language spoken by one of the men as he passes, I take a second look. I ask one of my co-workers who those men are, and he tells me that they are German Prisoners of War. They have been sent by the English soldiers guarding them to find work that will benefit the English government. I am struck by this situation. Not that long

120

ago, Germans were forcing us Jews to work in their factories and now they are being forced to work in English factories. It seems the tables have turned for them. I decide that I need to give them a piece of my mind and when I leave work, I yell obscenities at them in German. It makes me feel better to tell them how I feel. They are the prisoners now and I am finally free.

Rose and Max in Bedford, England, late 1946

CHAPTER TEN

Developing English Ways and Independence:
Rose

My English is getting better. I speak several languages, so learning one more, especially since it no longer has that heavy Scottish accent, is not too hard. It is four months since we arrived at Bedford and I practice talking in English with Max, Fred and another young man. I am pleased that I can now carry on a conversation.

One day, a counselor encourages me to look for a job, now that I can speak and understand English. I tell her I would like to work and we discuss options in the neighborhood. I decide to pursue a job in sewing, since Momma and Aunt Lea taught me to sew at home. I will feel close to my family when I sew, since Tata was a tailor and Aunt Lea sewed all our dresses when I was little. The next day, I go to the local garment factory to apply for a job sewing children's dresses. I get hired and enjoy working in the factory. It is close to the hostel, so I can ride my bike to and from work every day. I relish the ride because it gives me a few minutes alone to think before I start work. I love riding through the picturesque countryside, coasting down hill and stopping when and where I want along the way.

Sewing comes naturally to me and I like to talk with the other women as I work. Many times, people ask me about my experiences in the war. I usually don't know what to say. Most of the time I don't tell them how hard it was because I don't want to feel sad and don't think anyone else wants to get upset either. I strive to move on and start fresh, so I talk about my dreams and other things I like.

One day, on my way home from work, I stop at the drug store to buy a lipstick. As I stand in line to pay, a woman and her young son come up behind me.

"Why do you have a black number on your arm?" the small boy asks, tapping me lightly on my arm. I quickly look from son to mother and back again. My mind is racing. How could I tell a child about such horrors? "It's my phone number," I tell him. "So I won't forget."

His mother smiles at me with a knowing look and an appreciation that I considered the child's innocence before responding.

The boy smiles, and turns back to ask his mother about their dinner tonight. As she takes her son's hand and walks away, she turns and very gently smiles at me again as she nods. There is no doubt that she knows where I have been, since the community is aware of our hostel survivors' group. I am so relieved not to have to speak about the horrors I endured, especially to a child.

Max, Fred and "The Boys" survivor group in Bedford, England, 1946

CHAPTER ELEVEN

An English Man:
Max

As the winter of 1947 turns into the spring of 1948, my job at the truck factory is going well and I am now completely comfortable with English. Fred likes his job and his English has also improved. We talk daily of what will become of us now that we have good jobs and can speak the language. Everyone is talking about what their next steps will be. The hostel has been healing for us, but we have plans to move on. But are we ready to move away from our survivor friends?

Many of our friends have already moved to Canada, Australia, Palestine and the U.S. We promise to stay in touch with each other since we are now family. Fred and I decide to move to London where there may be more opportunities. Rose tells us she also wants to go to London. The three of us agree to make this our plan.

At the hostel, our billeting officer works to place refugees. He helps us find suitable homes in London. The Jewish Refugee Committee and the Committee for the Care of Children from Concentration Camps screen families willing to accommodate orphaned survivors by advertising in the London paper, *The Jewish Chronicle*. They inquire about the accommodation, spirit and Jewish culture in the household to best match the survivors to their host. Once a match is determined, the organization pays the host and connects them with the orphan.

I am placed with a young family with two kids. It is a kind and casual environment and I am thankful for my placement. It does not take long to find work at a car and truck manufacturer in the woodworking division. The company builds a variety of cars and trucks. We build vans for businesses and wooden station wagons. I even fit the wooden portions of cars being built for Queen Elizabeth. Every day I ride a bike to work and home. When it rains in London, as it often does, I wear a tarp over my clothes. I ride in the winter as well, sometimes through the snow. The wife at my new home makes me a sandwich for lunch every day as part of my rent. I do not care for the beet root or cucumber sandwiches she gives me but eat them daily as this allows me to save money. I now belong to a union, have a job I enjoy and make a good wage. It is hard to believe how far I have come in a year.

Fred shares a room with another survivor in a family's household. He works in a factory making parts for ships and saves money for the day when he will no longer live with a family, and can live on his own. Fred has become quieter since the war happened. Initially we both were quiet when we came to England, but I feel I became more like my old self over time. Fred still isn't quite his old self yet, but he willingly goes to work each day. He wears Dad's gold watch chain around his neck always. I see him sometimes touching it and looking off into the distance, lost in thought. I used to interrupt him when I saw this behavior, but now I leave him alone. Maybe that is how he processes the memories of what happened to him.

Rose shares a room with another survivor in a home with two kids. She seems so happy there. They all are good friends and she loves the children. Rose finds work in the garment industry. She is a competent seamstress, sewing children's clothes. Her life is stable and she seems happy. She, too, is saving for an even more independent living situation, free of all support systems.

Now that we are settled in London, the three of us join a group of survivors called the "Primrose Club." All survivors in London and the nearby vicinity are welcome to participate in the club's activities. We are a substantial group that meets regularly at a central location and often go out into the city for activities as well. We listen to music, dance, play ping-pong and go to movies together. During club events, I see Fred smiling and enjoying himself. It is wonderful to see him like that. Even young adults who are not survivors attend the fun events. It is a safe way to meet new people. We have a sense of community now with people we know and trust, and the group is expanding.

During this time, Rose and I get closer. I often ride my bike to visit her. One time it is so foggy when I leave her house in the evening, that I crash into a telephone booth. After a few minor adjustments, I brush off the gravel and ride my bike home. I realize Rose means something to me that I am willing to work this hard to see her.

Rose, Max, Fred and friends at their wedding in London, England, July 27, 1950

CHAPTER TWELVE

Our Adventure Together:
Rose

I dream of a life with Max, although I have not told him. It took me a while to understand my feelings, but now I am sure. I know Max is the one for me. I try dating other men, but none of them compare to Max in my eyes. Some of the other men are persistent, but they don't do anything for me. Max is approachable and would never say anything to hurt another person. He is one hundred percent honest and accurate about the things he says. He is considerate, so smart, and good looking too. For now, we are very good friends who live and work in the same city. He needs time, but I am certain: Max is "it."

When Max begins to seek me out in London, I think that his feelings may be changing. I could not be happier. It is a thrill to date him. He doesn't talk too much, but when he does, he says something deep and meaningful. He is so kind, and I enjoy all of our time together. We have many things in common and understand what each other has been through, situations that others cannot comprehend. We don't even have to talk about it, we just know. I believe something is happening between us.

Late in 1948, after a year of knowing each other, going steady and growing into adults, we have grown very close. One day, he surprises me with a beautiful diamond ring and asks if I will marry him. I am over-the-moon excited and accept immediately. I am so happy. Max explains how he had the ring made for me by one of our friends in New York, who now operates a jewelry store. Max chose the design and the stones, saved up and paid for it without me knowing anything about it. I love how romantic Max is.

It is hard to believe I can feel so much joy after having experienced so much pain. We cannot marry yet as neither of us have anything. We are both happy and motivated to save all we can to host a big wedding. No family members except Fred will be able to attend our wedding, which makes me sad, but it will still be a beautiful, happy occasion. We continue to work and have fun in the evenings and on weekends with our friends. Life is very good for us now. We enjoy making all the arrangements and planning for our new life together. We remain engaged and independent for nearly two years before we get married.

The big day arrives on July 27th, 1950, at the West London Synagogue, near Marble Arch. Our wedding is the first of the survivors' group and we are thrilled. It is a joyous occasion celebrating with all our survivor friends. Hugo Gryn, one of the boys from the hostels, is Max's best man and a sound spiritual advisor to both of us. He is studying to become a rabbi. Our sponsor and rescuer, Leonard Montefiore, walks me down the aisle in place of my father. Just before the ceremony, I think about my family. My mother, father, brothers and sisters are all missing from my big day. It hurts that my family cannot be here, but I know I must let that go. I will never be able to recover what the Germans took from me, but I can make a new family with Max and our survivor friends. I wear a beautiful white gown and walk down the aisle to join Max in his black top hat and tux. He looks so happy and handsome. All I can do is smile as I hold his hand and say my vows. We are a perfect pair and the ceremony is poignant for all to see: new life coming from the worst of adversity. Our reception is a catered dinner where 95 percent of our guests are survivors. It is a wonderful celebration and we spend all our savings to make it so. We are no longer fearful. We are full of hope for the future we freely create.

I am so excited to visit Paris for the first time for our honeymoon. The city is more beautiful than I had imagined and a wonderful beginning for our new life, filled with hope for the future. At the hotel, the concierge says that our room rental includes a continental breakfast. Neither Max nor I know what that means. The next morning, we decide that since breakfast is included, we should order everything on the menu. We feast like kings, laughing and talking for a long while before beginning our day. The rest of our trip flies past in a blur of happiness and adventure. I never thought I could be this happy again after all we lived through in the camps. As we head back to England, I think of my parents and wonder if they were ever this happy. Thinking of my parents makes me miss them and for a moment I am sad. But then we arrive at our destination, and sad thoughts are pushed aside in favor of hope for the future.

A few weeks later, we receive a bill from our Paris hotel. Confused, I read it aloud to Max. It takes a long while to read through all the charges, but by the end, Max laughs and turns to me saying, "Breakfast must not have been included after all."

I must look worried, because Max pats my hand and assures me not to worry as we will pay it off in installments. He writes to the hotel to establish a monthly payment plan. We laugh often about our honeymoon mistake, and always end saying it was worth it.

During our early days as a married couple, many more incidents like this occur. Each time we encounter a problem or make a mistake, Max assures me, "We'll figure it out, Rose."

When I get upset, he is always there to calm me down and make everything okay. Max reminds me: "If you can survive Auschwitz, you can survive anything!"

We begin our married life by renting a room from a local London family while we look for our own apartment. Eventually, we move into a furnished apartment and start our life together free of any support from the Jewish community and the English government. It makes us both so proud that we can support ourselves. Our road to independence, after all that World War II took from us, has been long and hard but we have finally made it. We love to entertain, something I never thought I would do. On Fridays, our single friends come over to play cards. It reminds me of Momma working in the kitchen with the other women from the village. They would laugh and talk as they cooked, kneaded bread or chopped vegetables. I hope that I am as gracious a hostess as she was. I miss my family often, but I am comforted by the fact that I am building a family here with Max. Our friends can never replace the people we lost, but they can occupy a new space in my heart.

London is a fun city for us. We have lots of friends, and enjoy our jobs. Five years have flown by since leaving the hostel and we are so happy together in our new life here. One night, over a wonderful dinner of fish and chips, Max proclaims: "Rose, I think it's time for us to move to America."

His statement takes me by surprise. Max periodically talked about moving to America since we met. We talk about America as a destination for someday, but I never considered that "someday" might be today. He told me that his father had been trying to get the family emigration visas before the Germans rounded up all the Jews.

"I don't know, Max. What will we do in America?"

"Whatever we want," he tells me with a smile.

How could anyone say no to that? America is the land of opportunity and I have always thought it would be fascinating to live there. I tell him that I just need time to process the idea. We talk about it several more times before deciding this is where our new life is leading us. I am ready to move to America! Though

Max grew up in a city, I am still adjusting to it. I am now finally accustomed to life in a place where there are no Gestapo hovering, watching my every move. I find the anonymity of the city almost soothing. I will miss all of our friends in London, but promise to keep in touch. I hope that life will only continue to get better as we start our next adventure together in America.

Rose and Max on Coney Island, New York, 1953

CHAPTER THIRTEEN

The Grand Plan—America: *Max*

After spending our first year of marriage in London, I work with my family members in the United States to obtain immigration visas for Rose and me. It takes many months, due to the health regulations put in place by the U.S. government. Because I had tuberculosis and typhus in Theresienstadt, the U.S. government makes me go through extra examinations since they do not want immigrants bringing infectious diseases into their country. I worry that we will not be able to get visas because of my health, but finally the doctors approve me and we wait anxiously for our documents.

One day in 1951, I return home after work and find that my cousin has sent us our visas. Rose and I are jubilant that our time has finally come for this new adventure together in America. For a moment, I am transported back in time 16 years. I can see Dad discussing American immigration visas with Mom. He wanted so badly to get them for us before it was too late. Unfortunately, the Germans took us away before our paperwork could go through. My dad's life-long dream, which I thought had died with him, is now coming true. We are going to America. For a moment, however, I am paralyzed with sadness. Fred, my closest living blood relative, will not be coming with us. He has chosen to remain in London, as he has a job and friends here. He says he will come later.

We spend several weeks planning for our departure. We gather our small amount of clothes and possessions into suitcases, selling to our friends what we cannot take with us. The day before we leave, I see Fred one last time. He comes over to our apartment and we talk about how proud Dad would be of us for moving to America and fulfilling his dream. We never discussed this before, so I am surprised when Fred brings it up. He gets a faraway look in his eyes and stops talking. Then he pulls something out of his pocket and I see that it is our dad's watch chain. He's had it since the camps, wearing it every single day as a reminder of what we lost. It has been with us through everything, witnessing our struggles and successes and encouraging us to keep going even though our dad couldn't.

"You will have better use for this than I will," he says, handing it to me. Maybe he is thinking, "Since you protected it in the camps for all that time, you are the reason we still have it. You are the one who rescued it."

Fred doesn't say anything else, but then again, he doesn't need to. We Schindlers don't talk much about our emotions. Dad was a stoic man, and neither Fred nor I are comfortable talking about feelings. Even though we don't speak them out loud, I can tell that we are both struggling, remembering the camps and our lost family as we look at one another for a silent moment. Finally, I thank him and close my fist over the chain. This is the only thing that remains of either my dad or my mother. It is the only connection I will have to them for the rest of my life. And it is a tangible connection to my brother Fred. In my twenty-two short years, I have never felt the wave of emotion that crashes over me now. I fasten the chain around my neck, where I plan to always keep it. Before he leaves that night, I hug my brother one more time. We know from experience that nothing in life is certain, and this may be the last time I see him. I tell him that I love him and he reciprocates before walking out the door without looking back.

The next day, October 3, 1951, Rose and I both wear our fathers' watch chains as we leave the apartment. We look back at the door of our first home together and know that memories of our families will live on with us in our new home in America. We make our way to the docks, where we board the SS De Grasse. I have never seen such a large ship. It is a classy French vessel, carrying many people across the ocean on its nine-day journey. They serve wine every evening with a dinner fit for royalty. For most of the trip, Rose is very seasick and spends all her time in our room. Though worried about her, I highly enjoy the voyage, relishing the sound of the ship cutting through the waves, leaving a wake of foamy white water behind. I explore the entire ship, feeling freer than I ever have before.

When we reach New York City on October 12th, my uncle and second cousins meet us at the dock and put us up in a Manhattan hotel for two nights. Our hotel window looks out onto a junkyard, which makes me want to check out as soon as possible. After a quick breakfast on our second full day in America, my uncle gives us twenty dollars and says, "Good luck. You are on your own."

From then on, we never stay with family again. I do not feel I need them. We can make it here in America on our own, as long as Rose and I have each other.

We find a survivors committee that helps us locate a room in a Brooklyn house with kitchen privileges for forty dollars a month. We have about twenty dollars in our pockets, so we both begin looking for work. I try to find a job in woodworking without much success. Eventually, I find a job as an assembly-line inspector with the Detector Scale Company which makes household scales.

At the same time, Rose finds work in the garment district sewing women's dresses. She rides the subway to and from the garment factory. When a friend tells her she can make more money at a different factory because she sews rapidly, Rose switches jobs. The friend was correct, as Rose sews one dress per day at first, but soon increases her pace to three dresses per day. She joins the Women's Workers Union and finds stability in her work. The factory closes for six to eight weeks each summer because there is no air conditioning. During those weeks, employees receive unemployment checks.

I am not happy at the scale factory and start searching the paper every day for a better job. I keep seeing International Business Machines (IBM) advertisements. I learn that computers are the thing of the future, and I want to be part of it. I attend night classes in computer technology, offered by IBM, to build my credentials and learn how to be an IBM tabulator. Once I complete the classes and get my certificate, I interview for computer jobs. The Royal Globe Insurance Company hires me and I am thrilled. It is wonderful to work in the financial district at the bottom of Manhattan, near Wall Street. My office is on the 15th floor where I shuffle, sort and collate IBM cards. I also learn to wire the machines that do the adding and subtracting.

After a time, we find out an apartment is open in the building my Uncle Izzy owns. Rose and I decide to move in to be near family. After having no extended family for years, it is comforting to spend time with them. I still miss my brother in London, but it is nice to have relatives close by. Rose would love to have her sisters nearby as well, but that is not an option. We move right next door to Aunt Toby and Uncle Izzy, who both speak English with heavy German-American accents. Because we have British-English accents, we can hardly understand each other at first. We often laugh trying to figure out what the other is saying.

Within a few years of our five years living next to our aunt and uncle, Rose and I start speaking with their German-American accent.

Our lives are full and happy. We decide to redecorate our apartment and have great fun acquiring new furniture and appliances.

Rose starts having difficulty with her teeth, experiencing a

lot of pain. Our dentist is surprised to find her teeth have been drilled out and filled with cement. Rose tells him this happened in Freudenthal. He is sorry to tell Rose that she will likely lose many of her teeth over time as a result. Initially, the solution is a partial plate on top, meaning that Rose will have several false teeth as she waits for the rest to fall out. While having a plate is not ideal, at least the pain is gone when she gets the partial plate.

One day in 1954, Rose is on the way home from work on the subway when she finds herself on the floor of the train, looking up. People gather around her and tell her she passed out. She cannot understand why this happened as they help her back up to a seat and give her water. I tell her to go to the doctor to see what is wrong, maybe this is related to her teeth.

Rose makes an appointment with our doctor and promises to call me at work when she knows more.

When Rose calls me the next day, she tells me there is nothing at all to worry about. Excitedly, she says, "The doctor says that the only thing going on with me is I am pregnant!"

She pauses and waits for my reply. We made sure not to get pregnant earlier because we had so little and could not support a child.

"Why, this is wonderful news! I will tell everyone we know! I am going to be a father and you will be a fine mother!"

We are both overjoyed.

Rose begins to plan the baby's room. This apartment has come to mean so much to us. It is the first place that we have been able to customize to our liking. Most importantly, this is the home where we have our first child, a daughter we name Roxanne. She is perfect and we could not be happier.

In 1955, I am busy working in the computer industry and enjoying it. My aunt and uncle encourage us to go west to California where there are unlimited opportunities. After discussing it with Rose, I contact Henry Zaks, a survivor friend we met in the UK who now lives in San Diego, California, and is in the military. I set up a visit to see him and explore job offerings in San Diego over my Christmas vacation.

The California weather is appealing and I am very pleasantly surprised to find many job openings for me. I interview at a few different places and accept an offer from a company called Solar within three days of arriving. The salary is double what I make in New York. I call Rose and tell her the good news, asking her to pack up the house and join me. Rose is always amenable to an adventure, but it is more complicated now. She is working, and we have a one-year-old. Rose says she will need some time to prepare, but is happy to begin again in California. Meanwhile, I remain in San Diego and buy my first car, an old Ford, to get to work and back. I am proud to own it.

Rose arrives in San Diego in April of 1956 with baby Roxanne and we stay in a hotel until I locate a cottage house for us in the neighborhood of North Park. Because Rose is ambitious, she is always looking for an opportunity to add to the family income. Within weeks, she finds a job at Golden State Fabrics where she sells fabric by the yard. The job is familiar to her and her schedule works for our family.

Shortly thereafter, I learn from a friend in our survivors group that there is a benefit we don't know about. It seems we can apply for reparations from Germany, as survivors of the Holocaust. We need to register with the German Embassy in Los Angeles. Rose and I make child care arrangements for Roxanne so we can drive up to Los Angeles to complete the needed paperwork. Although it can never make up for the senseless loss of our families and the unspeakable experiences in the camps, it does help to know that the German government is attempting to make amends for the wrongs they did. We help Fred, Helen and Judy get the paperwork they need as well, so they can benefit from this program too.

Rose, Max, Roxanne and baby Benjamin, San Diego, California, early 1958

CHAPTER FOURTEEN

Our Family Grows in California:
Rose

After packing up everything in New York and settling in San Diego, Max and I decide to try having another child. Luckily for me, I had no real issues during my pregnancy with Roxanne. I feel great, except for the ongoing challenges with my teeth. It is a relief that we have a compassionate dentist in San Diego who keeps coming up with new solutions for my cemented teeth. He has never seen anything like it before and tells me that it is likely that no one else has either. I have to wonder if the demand of bearing a child was a strain on my body, because I experienced near-starvation in the camps. The issues with my teeth got worse during my pregnancy with Roxanne. When I find out later that year that I am pregnant with our second child, I worry that the issues with my teeth will continue to worsen during this pregnancy.

We are thrilled when Ben arrives in 1957. Having a second child reminds me of my Italian coworker in the garment factory in London, who told me I need to have many children to make up for all the family members we lost in the camps. With a smile, I realize Max and I are on our way to building a big family.

Shortly after the birth of Ben, Max and I are pleased to buy a home in Allied Gardens, a family-friendly neighborhood. It has a yard for the children to play in and a two-car garage.

We were blessed with two more boys: Steve and Jeff. We are now a happy family of six. I continue to work part-time while raising our children. Max and I experience true joy parenting our children. It is the thing we hoped for most of all, after losing our families in the camps. Perhaps knowing horrible pain has helped us to experience this wonderful joy now.

As our family gets bigger, we move to a home in the Del Cerro community of San Diego. The neighborhood is filled with young families, all with three or four children. Neighbors know and support each other. The kids all play together, have sleepovers and go to school together. As I watch Roxanne chase Ben down the sidewalk, I feel I have come so far from just being a survivor. I feel contentment and I am fulfilled.

Sometimes it is a challenge to balance work and kids, but Max is so supportive and knows I enjoy working. When I am at work, Max watches the kids. When he is at work, I watch the kids. We create routines for ourselves that help us and the kids find a sense of normalcy. At our house, Monday is pasta night which is the kids' favorite. Since we both starved in the camps, Max and I believe that wasting food is a sin. Many families believe you need to clean your plate, eating everything you are given. Our philosophy is different. If you don't clean your plate, that is okay. It just goes in the refrigerator and is served again the next day. Each Friday night is our Shabbat dinner and synagogue time. Saturday is Max's day with the kids while I go to work. Finally, Sunday is family day, when we all do something fun together. We love taking the kids to the beaches, enjoy family picnics in Balboa Park, and attending our local survivors group get-togethers and company parties with Max's co-workers. My life finally feels like it makes sense.

Religion remains a perplexing topic for me, but for Max it is clear: we are Jewish. Our family joins a local synagogue and attends regularly. Faith is a part of our lives but not in the Orthodox way it was for me in Seredne, Czechoslovakia. We do not speak Yiddish at home and do not cook kosher foods. We enjoy celebrating Shabbat and the holidays. We send our kids to Hebrew school and they all have Bar Mitzvahs. When I was a child, girls were not allowed to have a Bat Mitzvah, but I am eager for Roxanne to have this experience that I could not. I am thankful that our children choose to be involved in the Jewish faith, but it is not compulsory at our house. The camps changed all of that for Max and me. Our faith is comforting, but not something we follow blindly like we did before. Occasionally, I still wonder if there is a God. How could there be with all the terror that happened to us and others? Surely God would not have allowed it.

When I think about this, it makes me angry. I ask myself why God would have allowed the Holocaust to happen and I never come up with an answer. I cannot sort out what I feel, so this question has to be put aside to allow me to continue with all of the good in my life. There are so many things we love about our lives, but Max and I both long for one thing that is still missing. It is our connection with family. Although we talk to Uncle Izzy and Aunt Toby in New York by phone, we have no immediate family in California. Fred is still in London, Helen and Judy are still in Eastern Europe. We correspond with them by mail but that is infrequent and inadequate. The USSR does not release people to move freely, so my sisters cannot come visit. In addition, Judy is married and raising a child with Bumi, in Seredne. Judy wants stability and predictability in her life. She is happy where she is. I am so sad about not being near Judy, but at the same time, I have to honor and respect her choice. She wanted to settle down and have the familial experience robbed from our parents. How could anyone take that away from her? Helen, however, is interested in coming to the U.S.

Max tells me Fred is happy with his life in London, working in shipbuilding and does not want to emigrate at this time.

Jeffrey, Steven, Benjamin and Roxanne, San Diego, California, 1965

CHAPTER FIFTEEN

Another Dream Comes True:
Max

My life feels so full and happy and I enjoy being a father, but still feel an empty spot in my life. I know it is related to my brother, Fred. I hated to leave him when we emigrated. He was certain he wanted to remain in London. Now I can help him in the U.S. if he will just come. It takes some coaxing, but Fred finally agrees to visit when I tell him there is a big shipbuilding company in San Diego. He can get a job there and live with us, or nearby. In 1959 he, at last, agrees to come. I am so happy to think he will be here with us.

145

When Fred arrives, we are both excited beyond words to see each other. It is so good to have him near me. As promised, I help him get an interview with NASSCO, the local shipbuilding company. NASSCO hires him right away. Fred decides to stay in the U.S. and see how this job works out for him. He stays with us for a short time and then is eager to get his own place. Fred loves the kids, but is used to a quieter life. He is 30 years old, a bachelor, and deserves a place of his own.

Fred is quieter than before the war. He still has times when he seems absent from the conversation, despite being with us. All of his hair is gone and he wears a wig. He tells me that his hair never came back after the hostel. Although we never talk about it, I have to wonder if they did experiments on him in camp, like they did with Rose's teeth. Rose doesn't remember them working on her teeth, so it is possible that Fred just doesn't recall. I know other people from our survivors groups who lived through the camps and never quite regained their former personality. Fred and I always had very different personalities, even before the war. Maybe Fred handles the experiences differently than I do. We don't discuss these things with each other. Instead, we talk about how good our lives are now.

We really don't talk about the camps much at all. Our friends don't want to hear about the atrocities and we don't want to relive them. Even in our survivors group, it is not a big subject. It is difficult to talk about losing absolutely everything: your home, your family, everything you own, even your family photos. For most Jewish families, the only people to survive are those who left Europe or hid. Our circumstances are rare. The odds of survival in a concentration camp were best if you had family with you. Those who did survive and returned home have no proof of ownership for what they used to own. Our few family photos come from other family members that managed to avoid the war, either in Israel, the U.S. or in hiding in Germany. They sent us the photos after liberation because they knew we had none.

In our home, the kids are still too young to hear of our camp experiences. We will wait until they are older. There is no need to traumatize them now. Even Rose and I have an unspoken agreement not to speak of it between us. We both understand and do not need to talk about it. We are focused on going forward, looking ahead and working on everything together.

In 1960, Helen, at long last, agrees to move to the U.S. Rose is overjoyed and sets forth writing to both the American and Russian government to solicit her release from the USSR. Helen has little to hold her in the USSR, but does have her sister, Rose, who eagerly seeks her release to the U.S. The process takes quite some time, but in the end, both governments agree to allow her to emigrate to the U.S. Helen, who is still living in Prague, is moving to San Diego! Rose and I are overjoyed to have her in our home.

Helen is a 35-year-old single, modern woman with high ideals. Rose says Helen is just like she was when they were kids. She remembers that Helen didn't want to be a dressmaker, despite learning the skills. She thought it was boring. She wanted a higher education, which was not a common choice for girls in those years. If the war had not come, she would likely have gotten that education, Rose is sure.

Rose recounts a story of how the local matchmaker found a boy for Helen. He rode into Seredne on a horse from the next village. Since there were no horses in Seredne, they were all impressed. The boy liked Helen and wanted the match, but it was not to be. The war changed the course of all our lives and they were never able to be together. In some ways, Helen remains that same girl now, despite everything. She laughs and says maybe he was not enough of a man for her.

Rose and I are concerned Helen is not liking San Diego much. We help her get a job as a bookkeeper. Helen doesn't mind the work. Rose works very hard to expose her to the beautiful scenery, the culture and vibrant nightlife. I introduce her to our friends and a few single men. San Diego is not a big city like Prague, where Helen feels comfortable. Despite thoroughly enjoying getting to know her niece and nephews, Helen wants something more. After six months, she decides to visit New York City, which is closer to her idea of a good fit for her. When she returns, it is clear she has fallen in love with New York, and wants to move there. We are sad that she won't be living near us, but we understand she needs to be happy. At least we can visit her in New York. Helen promises to keep in close contact and wants us to visit her often. With a heavy heart, we help her prepare to move.

Helen keeps her promise to stay in touch and clearly is very happy in New York. She tells Rose how her friend introduced her to a Holocaust survivor named Sam, from Budapest. Rose can hear in Helen's voice that she really cares for this man. She tells Rose how good he is to her and how she hopes he will ask her to marry him. On our next phone call, Helen tells Rose with great excitement that he did propose and she accepted. When we visit her, we see that Sam is so good to Helen and truly loves her. We are thrilled that Helen, who is 40 years old, is finally getting married!

In 1961, after five years at Solar, I take a job at General Dynamics and settle in quite well as a Tab Operator. I keep abreast of new trends and skills. I take computer classes in the evenings, because I see their widespread use as an inevitability. My new skills get attention at work, and I earn position changes and promotions. Over the years I become a Computer Analyst, Superintendent, Project Manager and Software Developer. Ultimately, I build the online computing division at General Dynamics. I never let my fourth-grade education in Germany stop me from lifelong learning and growth. I want my children to see that anything is possible with determination, hard work and an eagerness to learn.

In 1966, Rose has over ten years of experience in the fabric store and sees there is money to be made in this business. She speaks with me about opening our own store. I support the idea and recommend it be right in our neighborhood, to allow for the family's needs. So, in 1967, we open our own fabric store, called Roxy's Fabrics. Rose hires staff, keeping two employees in the shop at a time. Each day, I go to the shop after work, so Rose can pick up Jeff from the babysitter's, care for the kids and cook dinner for the family. I close the store at day's end, and then join the family at home. Our teamwork makes the store successful for ten years.

Schindler family at Steve's Bar Mitzvah, San Diego, California, 1972

CHAPTER SIXTEEN

A Play Changes Things:
Rose

In 1972, when Steve is 13 years old, he is cast as Peter in the play *The Diary of Anne Frank* at his middle school. During rehearsals, Steve tells his teacher that his parents are Holocaust survivors. I am surprised when the teacher asks if I might come and talk to the children about my experiences. If my son is willing to talk about our experience and his teacher thinks it is of value for children to hear, maybe it is time for me to talk about the Holocaust.

I agree to speak to the class. I stand up with my shaky knees and tell my story to the children, who are clearly moved. In that moment I realize that my story, told in person, has a unique value to children. I clearly hear my father's voice in my head, "Live so you can tell the world what they are doing to us."

Speaking to the children is how I can simultaneously honor my father's request and help to broaden their minds. I realize this is my gift to the world and a way to help make sure that events like the Holocaust never happen again.

After my presentation, the children in Steve's class write compassionate letters to me. They touch me to my core. I realize that innocent children are helping to mend my heart with kindness. They also speak of a desire to change the world, prevent problems that could lead to something as horrific as the Holocaust and a need to work together. If children can learn these powerful lessons from my experiences, they can change the world.

Something shifts in me. The story that has been so hard to believe, so hard to tell others, so hard to listen to, has a new value. I never put it behind me, I only set it aside so I could move forward. Now I realize it can change perceptions. That horrible tattoo that once robbed me of my name is my proof that I am telling the truth. The Germans did not succeed in their endeavor to silence the Jews, or prevent anyone from telling of their atrocities. I am one of the few who remain, and I can tell the world. A25893 on my forearm has a new value and I am not one to pass up an opportunity. This may be my first time speaking, but I will find more places to share my story.

I am excited to begin speaking to young people. Initially the invitations to speak are not often, as schools are not reading about the Holocaust, but eventually they begin to pour in. When I speak, I usually go alone. Sometimes I feel small and insignificant, but I always remind myself that even though I am just one five-foot-tall woman, I have a powerful story to tell.

Rose after presenting to Urban Discovery Academy, a K-8 school in San Diego, 2015

CHAPTER SEVENTEEN

A New Purpose Begins:
Max

"How did your talk at Steve's school go today?" I ask Rose as I hand her a mug of coffee. The children have gone to bed and she and I are finally alone in the kitchen discussing our day.

"It went well," she says. "I loved all their questions."

"What did they ask?" I inquire, thinking of my inquisitive son Steve and the types of questions he usually asks. My own questions often remain internal, but children ask their questions out loud.

"One student asked how we can prevent this from happening again. I told her we need to be aware that it really happened and it can happen again if we don't learn from this. Education about what happened is the solution to prevent it from happening again. I also wanted to give them some advice they could use today, in school. So, I encouraged them not to allow others to bully those who are less strong. Instead, speak up to stop bullying, because those who bully without redirection as kids become lifelong bullying adults. I ended with, 'we all have equal rights in this world, so be a good person to all people.' Choosing unity, diversity and peace in your life will give you great rewards."

"That's great. It is so true that education matters and concern for others will make the world a better place. I can see that this is quite rewarding for you," I say. "What else did they ask?"

Rose thought for a moment before responding.

"One child asked 'why do I think I survived Auschwitz?'" she says softly. The fact that a child asked this is interesting to me. Sometimes children say things that adults wouldn't. I know that Rose has thought about this before, so I am interested to hear her answer. I push her a little.

"And what was your answer?" I ask quietly.

"It's a miracle that I survived Auschwitz II-Birkenau. Also, I really do think part of it is because I kept looking out and trying new things. I wouldn't give up. I just continued and never gave up hope."

As I process her words, she squeezes my hand across the table and says, "You did the exact same thing."

This takes me aback for a moment. It is true, but I have never thought about my time in the camps in this way before.

"It really is true that you don't know when the next attempt at survival might be the one that succeeds," I say. I smile and squeeze her hand back. "You really are amazing, Rose."

"We got to this place together, Max," Rose replies before placing a kiss on my cheek.

We sit silently for a moment as we both ponder how our lives could have been different. Before this moment is broken, I squeeze her hand to get her attention. **We have climbed mountains I did not know we could climb. We made it, Rose! We made it!"**

Rose and Max at Girl Scout Campout, San Diego, California, 2016

The Later Years:
Rose and Max

The Schindler pair remained actively engaged in Holocaust activities for many years.

They continued to be members of the '45 Aide Society. This group maintained relationships with European survivors who became family after the war, when blood relatives were lost. Max and Rose have been steadily involved in The Butterfly Project, which was founded in San Diego in 2006. The Butterfly Project is a new approach to educating students about the Holocaust that honors survivors, while memorializing the 1.5 million children murdered with one ceramic butterfly painted for each child lost. For many years, Rose has also been the president of the New Life

Club, a local San Diego organization of Holocaust survivors.

After he retired, Max joined Rose at speaking engagements to share his story. Their over 40-year commitment to tell the world what happened continued. Together, they spoke to over 200,000 students and members of various branches of the military, as well as fraternal and religious organizations. They shared their forearm tattoos, A25893 and KL, with everyone. Rose always wore her father's watch chain, while Max shared proof of his internment in the concentration camps in the form of German documents. Rose fondly recalled after having been liberated and safely rehabilitated in Great Britain, "I fell in love with Max right away, but it took me a while to catch him," with a sparkle in her eyes. Their approachable manner was equally effective with children and adults. They continued to love the questions the kids asked and were shocked by how many of them don't know about this time in history. Those who heard their story left the talks broader in their thinking and wiser about life. When Max left this earth in 2017, with his beloved family at his side, Rose was crushed. Now in her late 80's, Rose continues speaking on her own, to honor both her family and his.

Both Max and Rose have been interviewed extensively by the news media over the years. Their video testimonies are included, along with 52,000 other Holocaust survivors, at the USC Shoah Foundation Institute. Steven Spielberg, who sought to document all testimonies of this horrific event, founded this organization after the success of his movie based on the book *Schindler's List*. This huge archive is accessible to all.

Max and Rose have earned many awards. They were honored to receive the Jewish Heritage Month Local Heroes Award from KPBS television in 2016. Rose was named one of the Cool Women of 2015 by the San Diego Girl Scouts, as well as a Woman of Valor during the 24th Annual Lipinsky Family Jewish Arts Festival in 2017. She was awarded an honorary high school diploma from La Jolla Country Day School on June 1, 2018, and an honorary M.B.A. degree from California International Business University on May 3, 2019. At La Jolla Country Day School the senior class unanimously voted to award Rose the certificate after hearing her speak at their school. She was interviewed on both days, and with a big smile told the reporters, "This was the best day of my life."

In 1995, Max and Rose returned to visit Auschwitz II-Birkenau and Theresienstadt with their daughter, Roxanne. While abroad, they also visited Rose's hometown of Seredne, which is now part of Ukraine. In 2015, they were invited to be a part of the 70th Anniversary of the Liberation of Auschwitz II-Birkenau. They traveled with their sons, Ben, Steve and Jeff. Among the group of approximately 100 Holocaust survivors at the 70th Anniversary event, Max and Rose were the only married survivor couple in attendance. Most survivors had already lost their spouses by this time. Each one of Max and Rose's return visits to the camps was a challenging and emotional experience. They felt like they were walking on the graves of those who did not survive. On their trip in 2015, they also visited Max's hometown, Cottbus, Germany, where Max received a hero's welcome and was honored to sign the City's official registry of visitors, das Goldene Buch der Stadt Cottbus.

Max and Rose's lost family members' names are engraved on two memorial walls. The first is in the US Holocaust Memorial Museum in Washington, DC. The second is in the Holocaust Memorial Garden at the Lawrence Family Jewish Community Center in La Jolla, California. The La Jolla wall includes the names of those lost whose families now live in San Diego. It is an important place for local family members and friends to celebrate the lives of those murdered during the Holocaust.

Max and Rose Schindler leave an indelible mark on the world, and we are grateful. Their resilience, tenacity, grace, hope and kindness toward a world that was not always kind to them is a testament of their strength and endurance. They both remained open and eager to befriend people throughout their lives. Max and Rose leave many pieces of verbal advice for us to ponder: "Indifference is the greatest evil, so act. Be bold. Stand up for those who cannot."

"Without memory there is no culture, society or future."

"Now it is up to you to make the world different. Be part of the solution. Keep telling the world our story, for soon we will not be able to."

It is the Schindlers' fondest wish that one of their children would continue telling their stories to young and old, encouraging them to learn about the mistakes of the past so they are not repeated. This book is a part of honoring that commitment.

America encourages dreams, where anything is possible. Max and Rose are proof that reaching your dreams is possible. Many people are not blessed with mentors who whisper into their soul that they can make a difference. But you can. The Schindlers have spoken. It is your turn to reply.

You can view many of Rose and Max's live interviews online at YouTube. For more information, please look them up under Rose and Max Schindler, San Diego. We invite you to explore TwoWhoSurvived.com to learn more.

Historic Family Photos

Rose's father, Solomon Schwartz, 1942

Rose's parents, Regina and Solomon Schwartz, 192

Solomon Schwartz (center) with his nephews, Hershey (left)
and Wolf Schwartz, Seredne, Czechoslovakia, 1937

Rose's brother, Fischel Schwartz (ri
circa 1940

Max's father and uncles (left-right): Itshe, Paul, Benjamin, Max and Nathan. Cottbus, Germany, 1921

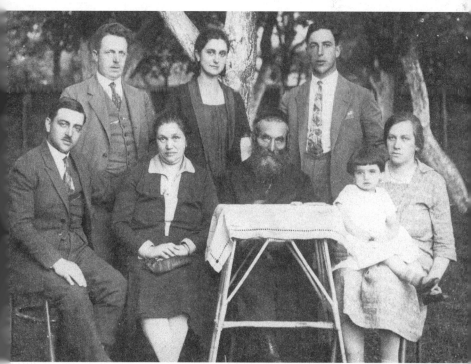

Max's parents, grandparents, and uncles (left-right): Uncle Paul, Uncle Nathan (wife Gusta), Rachela (Mom), Grandpa Simon, Benjamin (Dad), Grandma Yechil, Brezsko, Poland, 1926

Max's parents, Benjamin Schindler and Rachela Schweid's wedding in Brzesko, Poland, circa 1920

Max, Cecilia and Fred Schindler, 1933, wearing typical German lederhosen

Max's father, Benjamin Schindler, 1924

Max, Cecilia and Fred Schindler, Cottbus, Germany, 1935

Rachela Schindler (center) with Fred, Max and Cecilia picnicing at the river's edge
with cousins Esther and Max Kandel and their children, Cottbus, Germany, 1937

Solomon Schwartz, his niece Lenke Schwartz and nephew Wolf Schwartz, at Rose's home, Seredne, 1943

Schröder Wine Company owned by Uncle Nathan Schindler and the Baumwollspinner Family, 1933

Rose Schwartz (right) and friend Berta Weiss in Bedford, England, 1946

Rose and friends at Poulton House Hostel in Scotland, 1946

Max, Fred and friends, just four months after liberation, Windermere, England, September 1945

Rose (bottom row, second from left) and other survivors — the last transport from Prague to Scotland, Feb. 12, 19

Rose, Judy, Helen and friends two to three weeks after liberation, May, 1945

Rose's older sisters, Judy and Helen Schwartz, 1944

Rose's sister Judy and husband Bumi, 1955

165

Max Schindler, 1947

Rose Schindler, 1949

Rose and Max's wedding with Max's brother Fred, July 27, 1950

Anna and Benjamin Weiss sponsored Rose and Max, enabling them to immigrate to America

Joseph Bohm, Rose's uncle (see page 13)

Rose and Max in New York, 1953

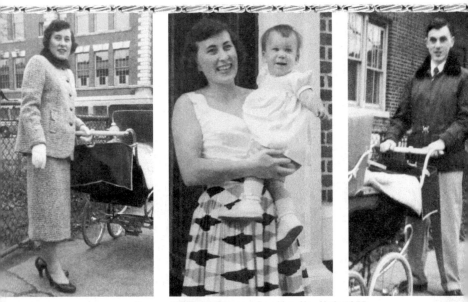

Rose and Max with Roxanne, Brooklyn, New York, 1955

Benjamin, Steven, Roxanne and Jeffrey Schindler, San Diego, 1960

Fred and Max, San Diego, California, 1961

Max and the kids, San Diego, California, 1963

Helen (left), her husband Sam (right) standing next to Rose, and cousins in Brooklyn, New York, 1972

זכור

Remember

As a proud testament to your generosity and as a permanent witness to your act of remembrance, the United States Holocaust Memorial Museum permanently acknowledges your support with the following words you have chosen, which have been engraved on the Donors Wall.

IN HONOR OF
THE SCHINDLERS AND SCHWARTZS

UNITED STATES HOLOCAUST MEMORIAL MUSEUM

WASHINGTON, D.C. · FALL 2002

SARA J. BLOOMFIELD, DIRECTOR

FRED S. ZEIDMAN, CHAIRMAN

Rose and Max at the opening of the United States Holocaust Memorial Museum (USHMM.org), signing the "Scroll of Remembrance" in Washington, D.C., April 1983 at the American Gathering of Jewish Holocaust Survivors.

The four Schindler siblings and their families donated to the United States Holocaust Memorial Museum to honor their family members who were killed in WWII with their names engraved permanently on the Donor Wall.

Memorial plaques enshrined at Yad Vasham's
Hall of Remembrance, Israel, 1994

Memorial stone of Rose's family members
who were killed during WWII, Prague

*Jeff, Rachel, Norm, Roxanne, Steve, Rose, Max, Amy and Ben at the unveiling of the Donor Wall
engraving at the United States Holocaust Memorial Museum in Washington, D.C., 2007*

Max and Rose in Prague's Old Town Square, Jan Hus monument, 1995

Stolperstein Memorial Stones outside Max's childhood home at 65 Calauer St. in Cottbus, Germany. They have been installed across Europe to remind people of the local victims of the Holocaust.

Rose and Helen with Dora Josipovitz (center, mentioned on page 64) and family, Los Angeles, 1985

Helen, Max's first cousin Rena, with Max and Rose, May 1999

Rose and Max Schindler's adult children - Jeffrey, Benjamin, Roxanne and Steven, San Diego, 1999

Rose and Max on their 50th Anniversary with their grandchildren, July 2000

174

Rose and Max with their grandchildren at grandson Jonny's Bar Mitzvah, September 2012

Rose and Max in 2012

Rose's 88th birthday party with her family, 2017

Rose's honorary graduation at La Jolla Country Day School in La Jolla, California, 2018

Rose speaking at The Butterfly Projec installation, 2018. thebutterflyprojectno

Rose and Max in late 2016

Rose speaking at an elementary school in 2019 at 89 years old.

Glossary

Allies: During World War II, the group of nations including the United States, Britain, the Soviet Union and the Free French, who joined in the war against Germany and other Axis countries

Arbeit Macht Frei: A German phrase meaning "work sets you free" that is known for appearing on the entrance of Auschwitz and other Nazi concentration camps

Brachot: Any one of the various Jewish benedictions

Central British Fund for German Jewry: Founded in early 1933 by a group of Anglo-Jewish community leaders, in response to the appointment of Adolf Hitler as Chancellor of Germany on a political platform of anti-Semitism

Challah: A special bread in Jewish cuisine, usually braided and typically eaten on ceremonial occasions such as the Sabbath and major Jewish holidays

Cheder: A traditional elementary school that teaches the basics of Judaism and the Hebrew language

Fachmann: Specialist, a person with specific knowledge in their field of expertise

Ghetto: Cordoned off, tightly packed areas of Eastern European cities established by the Nazis to confine Jews and Romani

Kapo: A privileged prisoner who served as a barracks supervisor/warder or led work details in a Nazi concentration camp

Juden Raus: German phrase meaning Jews Out, also an infamous anti-Semitic board game introduced in Germany in 1936

Kiddush: A ceremony of prayer and blessing over wine, performed by the head of a Jewish household at the meal ushering in the Sabbath or a holy day

Lager: German military name for camp or encampment. Nazis used this name in transit, labor, concentration and death camps.

Madrich: A youth leader, guide, trainer, educator or role model; someone who is an inspiration

Mikveh: In Judaism, a bath used for the purpose of ritual immersion

Muselmann: Slang term used among captives and guards of World War II Nazi concentration camps to refer to those suffering from a combination of starvation and exhaustion, seemingly resigned to their impending death

SA: Also known as Storm Troopers or Brownshirts, a paramilitary organization that used violence and intimidation to advance Hitler's rise to power.

Schnell: German for fast, or quickly

Shabbat: The Jewish Sabbath

Shochet: A person officially certified to kill cattle and poultry in the kosher manner prescribed by Jewish law

Shtiebel: A place for communal Jewish prayer that is smaller and less formal than a synagogue

Simcha: A Jewish party or celebration, a Hebrew word that means gladness, or joy

Sonderkommandos: The Jewish slaves in extermination camps that removed the bodies of those gassed for cremation or burial

SS: Schutzstaffel, or SS, were originally Hitler's personal bodyguards who took control of the police and security systems, forming the basis of the Nazi police state and the major instrument of racial terror in the concentration camps

Sukkah: A temporary shelter covered in natural materials, built near a synagogue or house and used especially for meals during the Jewish festival of Sukkot

Tzel Appell: A concentration camp roll call. Its purpose was not just to count the prisoners, but also to weaken, humiliate and intimidate. The prisoners would have to stand still for hours on end, wearing very thin clothing in all weather conditions.